Any Lengths

A Story Of How My Personal Journey Turned Into A Spiritual Experience

Mark Nodeen

the Peppertree Press
www.peppertreepublishing.com

Copyright © Mark Nodeen, 2024

All rights reserved. Published by the Peppertree Press, LLC. The Peppertree Press and associated logos are trademarks of the Peppertree Press, LLC. No part of this publication may be reproduced, stored in a retrieval system, transmitted in any form or by any means, electronic, mechanical, photocopying, recording, or otherwise, without prior written permission of the publisher and author/illustrator.

Cover Photography by Julie Ann Bakker
Graphic design by Elizabeth Parry

For information regarding permission,
call 941-922-2662 or contact us at our website:
www.peppertreepublishing.com or write to:
The Peppertree Press, LLC.
Attention: Publisher
715 N. Washington Blvd., Suite B
Sarasota, Florida 34236

ISBN: 978-1-61493-989-4
Library of Congress: 2024919936
Printed: November 2024

Manufactured in the United States of America

Introduction

My name is Mark and I'm an alcoholic. My sober date is 5/22/22 and I am a member of Alcoholics Anonymous. I do not speak on behalf of the program of A.A. in any way. The purpose of this book is to share about my experiences with recovery, in recovery and with the Big Book of Alcoholics Anonymous. This book also covers the lengths I have gone to in my recovery, as well as the lengths that I went to in my active alcoholism and drug addiction. My hope is that you will find something useful in this book to help you along in your journey in life.

Greets, are to be received in each of A.A.'s two premier countries. South Africa nearly survey 50 groups carry-and 58 of the provinces on the African continent, making on the African communities on the African continent, and making America, Australia and Hawaii. All old timers are just now beginning to South Africa. Some are just now taking beginning have been made in some are just now taking a letter in Asia. Many of our friends overseas, only the company saying that this is but a beginning, only the country a much larger future ahead.

The spark that was to flare into the first A.A. group was struck at Akron, Ohio, in June 1935, during a talk between a New York stockbroker and an Akron physician. Six months earlier, the broker had been relieved of his drink obsession by a sudden spiritual

iv

Dedication

Dedicated to my little savior, Miranda; to my sponsor, George B.; and to my dear friend, Volunteer Alex.

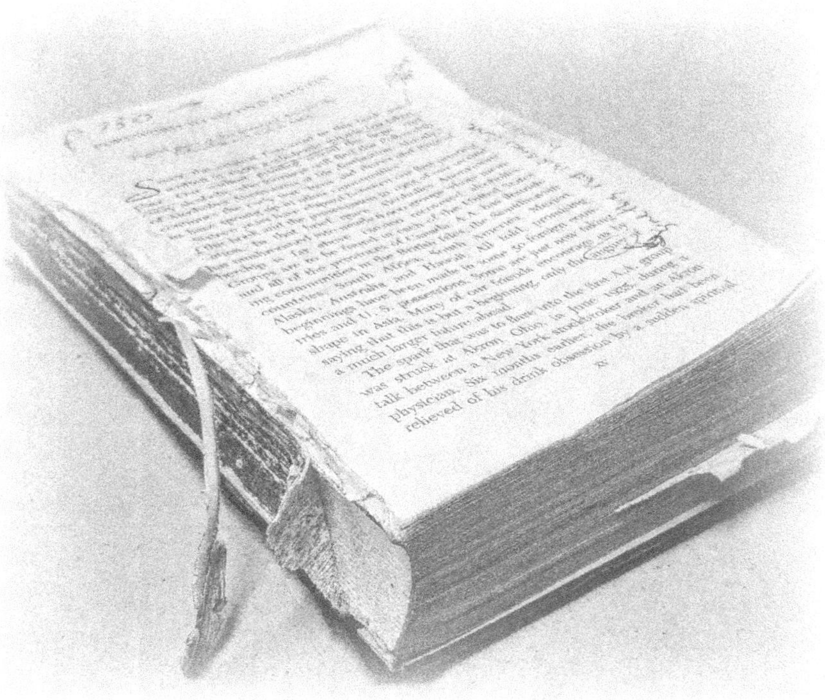

Foreword

Gratitude is an action word. The more I learn, the less I know. Funny how a little time in the AA program produces changes in ideas, emotions, and attitudes. I spend moments reciting pages out of AA literature, being inspired by eighty-year-old stories, and finding solutions to the challenges of life.

My Higher Power is also a crossing guard and gives me directions at intersections in my life. One day He graced my path with a fellow traveler on this road in recovery. It's special to see the onion of sobriety peeled back to reveal so much about each other. Mark was directed into my life to help foster spiritual growth in the both of us as we emerge into the Sunlight of the Spirit. The 12 Steps, to me, trigger, ignite, and fan the flames of spiritual growth.

What a blessing it is to see Mark allow this phenomenon of a spiritual awakening give his life purpose. He is totally different from the person I met at the intersection of Sobriety and Recovery, like in "Bill's Story" in the *Big Book*, page 11. Never mind the musty past—here sat a miracle directly across the kitchen table. He shouted great tidings. I saw that my friend was much more than inwardly reorganized. He was on a different footing. His roots grasped a new soil. I'm grateful to be a witness to a miracle. Thank you, God, AA, and Mark.

George B.

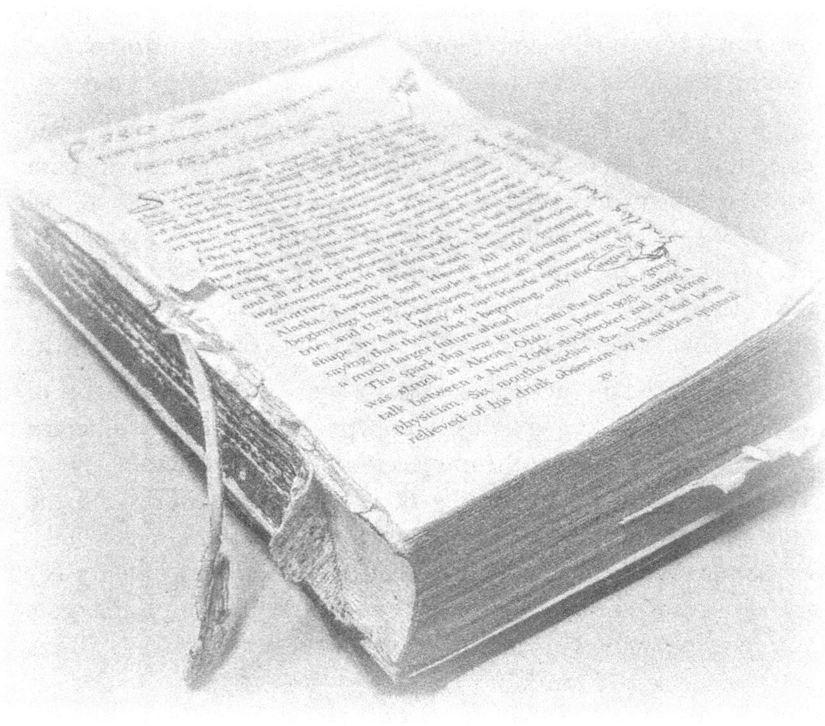

Table of Contents

Foreword iii
Chapter One - The Problem 1
Chapter Two - The First Step in Recovery 7
Chapter Three - Step 1 13
Chapter Four - Step 2 17
Chapter Five - Step 3. 22
Chapter Six - Step 4. 27
Chapter Seven - Step 5. 40
Chapter Eight - Step 6 & 7 44
Chapter Nine - *The Big Book* Breakdown with
   William D. Jessworth MD, aka Doc. 52
Chapter Ten - Steps 8 & 9. 58
Chapter Eleven - Step 10. 68
Chapter Twelve - Step 11. 73
Chapter Thirteen - Step 12 79
Chapter Fourteen - Seasons and Reasons 86
Chapter Fifiteen - The Spiritual Awakening. 98

Circus, are to be found in all the States of the Union, the provinces of Canada, and in Alaska, Hawaii and several foreign countries. South Africa, Australia and some of the Scandinavian countries, Central and South America, are just now taking shape. Beginnings have been made in Greece, Finland, Holland and behind the Iron Curtain. Many of our friends overseas are making strides in Asia. Many of our friends, only the first A.A. groups are a beginning. Some are just now taking shape. We know that this is but a beginning, only the start of a much larger flare that is to flare into the future ahead.

The spark that was to flare into the first A.A. group was struck at Akron, Ohio, in June 1935, during a talk between a New York stockbroker and an Akron physician. Six months earlier, the broker had been relieved of his drink obsession by a sudden spiritual

Chapter One

The Problem

"But, Doc, what about the voices in my head?"

These were the words that I managed to spit out of my mouth to the psychiatrist sitting in front of me. During the two years prior to this statement, I had managed to take my life from OK to *not* OK.

My life had been going smoothly up till this point—or so I thought. I was successful—I had a wife, a daughter, a home, and the accolades of many. I was at the top of my industry in woodworking, I had been in several magazines and news articles, and was known by many in my field.

In 2017, I hit the peak of my success and I remember clearly when a certain thought crossed my mind. I was thirty-nine at the time and about to hit forty. I was out with my wife at a movie, when this thought said to me, "Hey, go see your friend that you haven't hung out with in a while, and go partying! You deserve it! Ring in the last year of your thirties like a champ."

I had this friend whose nickname was, "Half Day." He earned that name while I was working with him on some jobs, because he was never on time. He always had some excuse as to why he was late. It was always an entertaining and wild story. He was funny and I liked him, so we had times where we hung out and got along fine. However, we also had times where we didn't speak for months on end, so it was time I reached out to him.

If anyone could party like I could, it was this guy! I called him and we linked up. I had missed him and his stories, and we picked up right where we left off the last time. He always had party favors and I knew he would be a great hookup for those things, so I could party hard till I hit forty. That was the plan in my head.

Now up to this point, I had periods in my life where I partied, but always managed to control it. I also would have periods of different experiences. I would go through phases of drinking and not drinking, only smoking marijuana and not smoking it, only doing ecstasy or molly and not doing either, only doing Xanax or not doing it, only doing meth or not doing it, only doing cocaine or not doing it, and on and on. Also, I had periods where I would combine a couple of substances for a while and then quit. I partied hard, but always managed to stop when I needed to. This time, it was going to be the same ... or so I thought.

The *Big Book of Alcoholics Anonymous* talks about this on page 31 in the second full paragraph (or at least a similar version of this).

I ended up partying with him and everything went smoothly for a while—we were the "Wrecking Crew" for a few months. We even took one of his buddies along for the ride for those short few months. The three of us tore it up. Every weekend and even during the week we were out on the town shutting the bars down, laughing, partying, and going all out. However, I was handling my work well and still able to keep up.

Good thing, too, because at this point in my life, I was busier than ever. At the woodshop I was a workaholic. I had projects coming out of my ears, so much so that I could barely keep up with it. My new friends were there to support me whenever I needed a pick-me-up. That's when I started to use cocaine as a way to work longer hours. I also had the funds to purchase a nice-sized bag multiple times a week for those long work days and work nights. Cocaine kept me going.

As I said earlier, I had always partied, but this was the first time in my life that I started to use so I could stay awake for work purposes. I noticed my hands would move faster, I could get projects done faster, and do it for two or three days on end till I had to rest. My, how the money flowed in and I was more successful than ever. I felt like a giant—the effect was astonishing.

Our AA *Big Book* talks about "The Effect." On page xxviii of the "Doctor's Opinion" in the last paragraph it says, "Men and women drink essentially because they like the effect produced by alcohol." Then if I go up to the first full paragraph on that page, the second sentence says, "These allergic types can never safely use alcohol in any form at all."

If I look back at my life, that is the way it has been, my whole life. This time, the disease that centers in my mind took a new form and money had become my God. When things were good, they were good, and when things went south in my life, they *really* went south. I used drugs to fuel my workaholic life and alcohol to come down at night. When life blew up in my face, I turned to the only stuff I knew I could use to cope—drugs and alcohol.

I loved the effect. I remember very visibly the first time I drank. My first drink was either a beer—Red Dog or an Ice House. I'm not sure which, but I do remember I hated the taste of beer. I did what any good starting alcoholic would do—I mixed it with soda. I believe it was root beer or something. I still hated how it tasted, but the effect blew me away. Immediately I forgot about all my pain as a teenager. I'll talk about that later, but the important part is the effect. Looking back, it had always been about the effect for me.

At this point in my life, after I was a workaholic, my friend, "Half Day," had departed from my life again, so I ended up reconnecting with another old friend of mine whom I knew partied like I did. He was a great dope man and was now back in my life. I was very happy, because I really needed that fix, since my business had just blown up in my face. My main client pulled the plug on their account, so I was left with almost nothing, which was my fault.

We had put all our eggs in one basket, and I was burnt out from over-working. We went down to just two clients—my friend's design firm and this one main client. When my main client pulled the plug, I watched everything we had been working for go up in smoke. I was too burnt out to dig deep for the motivation to step back, put in the extra effort to get the old clients back, and just move forward. I was frozen.

Drugs and alcohol unfroze me temporarily and my newly returned friend in life had all the supplies that I could handle. My use skyrocketed, and my work life decreased. I was adjusting my life to fit my habit, all while justifying the reasons. I played such a great victim. The year was 2020 and I had been using and drinking heavily since 2018—all in the name of success. However, my intent was wrong the whole time.

Well, by the time my wife suggested I was out of my mind, she had no idea what was going on. All she knew was that I was going crazy. It was suggested that I go back to therapy, so I did. I saw the therapist we had as a family. I told her what was going on in my head and the next thing I know, I was being referred to a psychiatrist.

My wife was a good woman and she went with me to that first appointment with the psychiatrist. I've always hated doctors—I still do to a certain extent. I had always been afraid that it was going to be the worst news ever when they talked to me. Never has it been that way, but I get all up in my head about it. We walk into the office waiting room, and I go to the bathroom to do the biggest rail of cocaine I've ever done. My justification was that it would calm my nerves. What it really did was put me out of my mind. I was in full psychosis by this time.

We sit down in front of the psychiatrist and without a proper diagnosis, drug test, or anything else, she asks what was going on. I told her some things that were going through my head and that sentence I spoke at the beginning of this chapter just came out of my mouth. She immediately gave me a cocktail prescription—for schizophrenia, of course.

Holy crap, did I have a good wife at the time! She made sure my drugs were laid out every morning, and every night, and that I took them. The medicine made me a zombie. The crazy thing is that I knew I was in psychosis, but on the flip side, I was still in denial about my addiction and my drinking. I didn't stop that either while I was on the medicine.

I had to curb the zombie feeling—it was a deadly cocktail. I was told to make sure my scripts were filled and I had regular appointments with the psychiatrist. My wife made sure I went. She was just doing what she thought was best for me. When I had that moment of clarity in May of 2022, a voice in my head said, "Now is the time to come clean and go to treatment!"

I had stopped taking those meds and spiraled completely out of control. I had hit pitiful and incomprehensible demoralization. I had gone to great lengths to hide what was really going on, but I hit my breaking point. My solution wasn't the solution anymore. On page 103 of the *Big Book,* last paragraph, it says, "After all, our problems were of our own making. Bottles were only a symbol." My problem went much deeper than that bag, those pills, and that bottle.

After exiting treatment in July of 2022, I had this ignorant thought that I could go through sobriety alone. I wasn't really into the meetings or getting a sponsor. I had tried, but I couldn't seem to find the right sponsor for myself. Besides, every time I looked at those steps printed on the walls in the meeting rooms, they scared me. I thought doing the steps was simply reading them off the wall and thinking about them.

Because of that thinking, I had an off-the-wall program. The further away I was from a drink or a drug, the more restless, irritable, and discontent I became. On page xxviii-xxix, in the "Doctor's Opinion," of the *AA Big Book,* it says, "They are restless, irritable, and discontented, unless they can again experience the sense of ease and comfort which comes at once by taking a few drinks—drinks which they see others taking with impunity."

This I know to be true firsthand. There came a point where it was do or die for me. I heard a guy in the meetings say once, "My sponsor said to me, DO THE STEPS OR DIE!" I used to think that was ridiculous, but I didn't know what he meant. I now know what he was talking about. I was dying inside slowly.

At this point in my book, I will lay out how I found my sponsor and what I looked at during the steps. Also, I will share with you how I continue to apply the steps in my life, so that I may continue to stay sober and in recovery. It is my hope that my experience might help the newcomer or the person going back through the steps. So let's jump into it.

Chapter Two

The First Step in Recovery

When I found my sponsor, I had already been through two sponsors. The first was basically a sponsor in name only, while the second was a "*Big Book* thumper" and he helped me, but in the end, he didn't have what I wanted. I knew this to be true, because by this point, there were a couple of guys in one meeting that pulled me to the side and asked an important question, "How do you know what you want, if you don't know what you want?" they asked.

That took me a minute to grasp, but it made sense. I had zero idea of what I was looking for in a sponsor, because I didn't know what I was seeking internally. They suggested that I make a "mission statement," and lay out what I was hoping to get internally from recovery. I took that suggestion and found myself writing things like peace, serenity, and no more chaos. They looked at it and basically said to use that list to go find my sponsor. I did exactly that.

I ended up finding a man who was unshakeable, because he had unshakable faith. I watched him for about two months talk the talk and walk the walk. I got to know him casually, before I finally got up the courage to ask him to sponsor me. He always wore a smile on his face and was the definition of happy, joyous, and free.

When I asked him to sponsor me, he looked at me and the smile fell from his face. Then he became really serious and said, "Yes." I immediately thought, *What did I just do?* I was inwardly afraid, yet still outwardly a little defiant, too, but ready for the work finally.

I was ready, because people had started saying things to me like, "You look like you need a fourth step!"

My response to that was, "Why? I'm happy, joyous, and free!"

Their response to that was basically, "Yeah, well, tell your face that!"

They were right. I did need some quality in my life. All I had was sobriety. I had heard someone in a meeting say, "You're either a spectator or a participant in AA." I took that as just not drinking, going to meetings, and reading or sharing in meetings. I now know what he meant. I have to participate in my own recovery by doing all the things that fit into the program of recovery, if I want a quality life. This included working the steps.

Now that "*Big Book* thumper" that I talked about did two things for me for which I'll forever be thankful. First off, he drilled the "Doctor's Opinion" into my head. He called it the "meat and potatoes" of the program. He is right—it is. It's how I diagnosed myself as an alcoholic. He kept asking me as we read it how I thought it applied to me. We also kept talking about situations from my life that applied to it.

Then he took me to page xxvi, end of the first full paragraph where it says, "In our belief, any picture of the alcoholic that leaves out this physical factor is incomplete."

He asked, "Is that you?" When I said yes, he proceeded to tell me, "Great, then any program that leaves out the spiritual factor is incomplete, too!"

Then he took me to page 86 of the *Big Book* and had me read "upon awakening" every morning, and "when we retire" every night. He knew what I didn't know—that I needed to build a conscious contact with my Higher Power.

I had a conscious separation from that power most of my life. I took the suggestion and it helped me get through till I found my official sponsor. Those two simple suggestions started to save my life. Without those simple tools, I think I would have relapsed in my early recovery. I still hadn't raised the white flag completely though.

When I connected with my current sponsor, we started reading the *Big Book* and the "Doctor's Opinion." I started making a list of things I wouldn't do if I was in sound mind—things that I did in the pursuit of my high or next drink. Some of those things go like this.

1. **Hang with the dopeman and make him my best friend.** Towards the end of my run, the dopeman was my "best friend." I put that in quotation marks, because now that I am in sound mind, of course, the dopeman was my best friend. I spent all my time with him, neglected my family, my daughter, and my obligations in life. He supplied me with what I needed and I supplied him with what he needed—money. I remember when he bought a new car and I was struggling to survive. He was showing it off to me and all I can remember thinking was, "Wow, I could have bought myself a new car."

2. **Judge others and call them alcoholics and/or addicts.** I used to sit at the dope hole and think to myself, "Wow, that guy is back for a third time today—what an addict!" All the while, I was forgetting that I had been there for three days straight. I would see someone bringing something to trade for drugs, like speakers or an IPad, and I would say, "Wow, what a junkie! I would never do that." However, I started doing that same thing under the guise of "I don't wear that watch anymore, so I have no use for it."

3. **Pawn things for money.** The mind is a wonderful thing. I could trick myself into believing almost any lie. I started pawning my things for money under the guise that I didn't have any use for them anymore. It started with my guns, because I didn't go shooting anymore. Next, it was my music equipment, because I wasn't in a band anymore and didn't play like I used to. Then instead of saving the

money, I would go pay my drug debt and buy more with the leftover. I had great credit with my dealers. I always paid on time and my credit line was infinite. When it came time to pay, I had plenty of things to sell to get the money. The last was my watch collection. I hit a period in my life where I loved watches. I had a Rolex Air King that I loved, which brings me to my number four.

4. **Steal from the dopeman.** So here is my stealing from the dopeman story—or did he steal from me, and then I just took back what was rightfully mine? You decide. I had this Rolex Air King that I absolutely loved at one point in my life. He would always say how bad ass that watch was. Eventually towards the end of my run, it was one of the last things I had left to sell, so I traded it to him for a bunch of blow and a thousand dollars. That thousand dollars was a down payment on it. He was going to pay me another fifteen hundred down the road.

Some time went by and he never paid me. I was still hanging out with him, all while buying cocaine from him in cash. I wanted him to pay me and he had excuses as to why he couldn't. I couldn't argue with him though, because he was one of my sources. He had this girlfriend and they would argue constantly. Whenever I was over at their house it was my favorite reality show. I would sit on the couch with popcorn and watch them fight. I would even instigate it, so I could watch the drama.

One night we were out and he hadn't been home in three days. His girlfriend trashed the apartment out of spite while she was drunk. He sent me over to his place to check on things and she was sick from the alcohol. She was throwing up and a friend of ours was attending to her. The dopeman called me and asked if I could find his money and the Rolex, as those two things were there in the apartment. He could have cared less about her. So I found the money and the watch. I returned the money to him but told him I couldn't find the watch. Now when I said the place was trashed, it was really destroyed. There was no way he was going to find that watch.

They made up a few days later and he searched for that watch for weeks. He couldn't find it. I had it and I went and resold it to a watch shop. I still had the box and paperwork, because I never gave it to him in the first place, and I got top dollar for it. I went and spent the money on drugs with his competition, because I was mad that he never paid me for the balance on the watch. I kept asking him if he ever found the watch, but he would say no. I told him he needed to pay me anyway, because it wasn't a "me" problem that he had lost it. He ended up paying me the balance, and I spent that money on drugs with his competition again. I don't think I would have done any of that, if I was in sound mind. I miss that watch—it was my favorite timepiece.

5. **Neglect spending time with my daughter.** I love my daughter. When I was on my run, she would ask me to spend time with her. I would say that I would, but my drinking and drugging came first. If I was too hung over on the weekends and we had plans, I would tell her I was too tired and wiped out from work. If we did spend time together, I would cut it short, so I could drop her off at home and go get my fix.

These five things are a small portion of the many things I did in the pursuit of my alcoholism and addiction. I don't think "normal" people act like this. Page 20 of the *Big Book*, the next to last full paragraph, talks about the differences between the moderate drinker, the hard drinker, and the alcoholic. The moderate drinker can take it or leave it alone. At one point in my life, I could do that. Then I became a hard drinker, and somewhere during this journey, I became an alcoholic.

Page 30 of the *Big Book*, in the chapter, "More About Alcoholism," the second full paragraph states: "We learned that we had to fully concede to our innermost selves that we were alcoholics. This is the first step in recovery"

A person in the program once asked me, "Are you an alcoholic?" I said I was an addict and he replied "Well, is there anything you could ever do un-alcoholically?"

Come to think of it, no there wasn't—not work, not money, and not women, TV, video games, collecting things, alcohol, or drugs. The list goes on and on.

That question, paired with the *Big Book,* paired with this never-ending list of things I did in the pursuit tells me one thing: Yes, I am absolutely an alcoholic to my core.

Chapter Three

Step 1

We admitted that we were powerless over alcohol—that our lives had become unmanageable.

When I acquired my first sponsor (in name only), he asked me if I was powerless, but I had zero idea of what that meant, so I agreed, just to shut him up. When I got my *"Big Book* thumper" sponsor, he asked me the same thing and, of course, I said, yes, but I still didn't fully know what that meant. However, this time around with my current sponsor, we talked about it in detail. Now that I had raised the white flag and conceded to my innermost self that yes, I was an alcoholic, a real alcoholic, I should probably understand powerlessness and what it means. If I don't, then I'm screwed. This is the step I have to do perfectly and do it right all the time. My goal is to become best friends with this step. *Step 1* is about quantity, while the rest are about quality, as my current sponsor says.

There is a great book out that I find pairs nicely with my *Big Book*. It's by a gentleman named Danny Falcone and is called, *The 20 Most Misunderstood, Misinterpreted, Mistakes of the Big Book of Alcoholics Anonymous*. On page 38 of his book, the first full paragraph says, "When you do what you already know you don't want to do, what you've sworn you'll never do again, but you do it anyway, that's powerless."

Now if I take what he wrote and turn to page five of "Bill's Story" in the *Big Book*, fourth paragraph, there is a perfect example of powerlessness. It says, "I woke up. This had to be stopped. I saw I could not take so much as one drink. I was through forever. Before then, I had written lots of sweet promises, but my wife happily observed that this time I meant business. And so, I did. Shortly afterward I came home drunk. There had been no fight. Where had been my high resolve? I simply didn't know."

If I look back at my run, that describes my powerlessness perfectly. How many times did I say to myself or others, "This is the last time." Then, I would go right back out and do it all over.

I clearly remember that feeling. It's 3 am. I am out of alcohol, I am out of drugs. I can't get package from the bar, nobody is selling liquor. I have zero drugs at the house and my dopeman is out, unreachable or I'm cut off, due to doing too much. Then pitiful and incomprehensible demoralization sets in, "How did I get to this point again?"

I become remorseful. I drink Nyquil or alcohol to hopefully pass out, with a resolution that this is the last time. Then I would wake up the next morning, sometimes ordering my fix immediately from one of my dealers, or I would do fine till about noon.

Sometimes I would order while crying to myself with my hands shaking, or I would just say, "Screw it! I can't make it." Then I would just order it, telling myself that tomorrow, I could quit. Or better yet, I would go to the dopeman's house, with a firm resolution that I wouldn't use or drink. I would be hanging out and a drink would be offered to me. I didn't want to be rude by saying no. Then I would end up buying a bag to go. I would hate myself until that first line of cocaine kicked in then I would say to myself, "I'm OK." I knew I wanted to stop and sincerely wanted to stop. Now that I understand powerlessness, I now know why I couldn't.

Danny goes on to explain in his book on page 38, first full paragraph, about the results of being powerless. The "Once I start, I can't stop," or "I can't control it!" makes a lot of sense to me. Those nights at 3 a.m. were painful. The "Disease of More" is painful. The unmanageability in this step, I associate with all the times I couldn't live without something in my system.

Yes, I had unmanageability in other areas, too, like finances, work, and relationships. I still do to this day, to some extent. It's almost as if page 52, second full paragraph of the *Big Book,* was right. It says, "We were having trouble with personal relationships, we couldn't control our emotional natures, we were prey to misery and depression, we couldn't make a living, we had a feeling of uselessness, we were full of fear, we were unhappy, and we couldn't seem to be of real help to other people."

I felt like this before my run, during my run, and after my run. I drank and used, as I was maladjusted to life. I couldn't roll with the punches and changes life threw at me, then I couldn't live without my solution. My unmanageability just piled up in all areas of my life and took on different forms.

As I was leaving treatment in 2022, they asked me a very life-changing question, "What are your chances of relapse?"

I said with confidence, "ZERO!" I wrote a sweet promise going out those doors of treatment and back into the real world. I picked up that attitude from the others in treatment, swearing up and down that this was their last time and they would never use or drink again. I hopped on that bandwagon. It was ignorant and cocky of me to write that promise without realizing what powerlessness truly was.

I was cocky in thinking that I could make it through life on my own without using or drinking again. Many of those who I was in treatment with did end up relapsing. They didn't work a program when they got out of treatment and went right back out. Now, I'm not ripping on treatment in any way. It was a great place to be separated from the alcohol and the drugs. I started looking at myself. It also allowed my ego to recharge and inflate again.

Page 101 of the *Big Book* says in the second full paragraph, "In our belief any scheme of combating alcoholism, which proposes to shield the sick man from temptation is doomed to failure. If the alcoholic tries to shield himself he may succeed for a time, but he usually winds up with a bigger explosion than ever. We have tried these methods. These attempts to do the impossible have always failed."

That explains so much in such a short statement. All the times I said I would stop and then sleep the weekend away in my isolated office, in the dark, in a weak attempt to detox. Then I would wake up on Monday morning to give up that "never again" statement I made a couple of days prior for a fix that I knew I didn't want, but had to have. That statement makes perfect sense. Now my hat is off to anyone who can leave treatment, not work a program and stay sober. Yes, there are people out there like that. But now that I've fully conceded to my innermost self that yes, I am an alcoholic, and if I don't do this first step, apply it every day, and continue to work a complete program of action, then yes, I am going to relapse.

I heard a speaker once say that there are two types of denial: one about the problem and one about the solution. I now know that I had been in denial about the problem, and for some time in early recovery, I was in denial about the solution. First, it was that sweet promise of the chance of relapse being zero. Then again, about these steps in the *Big Book*, I used to think that these steps weren't going to work, because they weren't my idea. I didn't come up with them. Then again, when did my ideas about how to stay stopped ever work? When did my plans and designs ever really work? All the times I isolated, all the sweet promises, and then in early recovery with my way of going to meetings, and how I looked at this program of recovery.

There is alcohol everywhere in this world and drugs are easily accessible. Just because I got sober doesn't mean the world is going to stop their drinking and drug use. If I am going to make it through this life sober, I am going to need some help—help from a power greater than myself, my sponsor, and the fellowship.

Chapter Four

Step 2

Came to believe that a Power greater than ourselves could restore us to sanity.

In early recovery, I kept hearing about insanity in the rooms being defined in a couple of different ways. One definition of insanity is doing the same thing over and over again and expecting different results. Another way I heard it explained was doing the same things over and over again, knowing what the results would be. In Danny Falcone's book, I absolutely love his definition of insanity.

On page 48 of his book, he says: "Sanity is the ability to see the truth about myself. Insanity is the *inability* to see the truth about myself." That explains so much.

On page 55 of the *Big Book* in the "We Agnostics" chapter, second full paragraph, it says: "Actually we were fooling ourselves, for deep down in every man, woman, and child, is the fundamental idea of God. It may be obscured by calamity, by pomp, or by worship of other things, but in some form or other, it is there. For faith in a Power greater than ourselves, and miraculous demonstrations of that power in human lives, are as old as man himself." Then it goes on to elaborate on that.

When I started into *Step 2* with my current sponsor, he asked me to do something simple, yet challenging. He had me make a list of ten attributes of my Higher Power. This wasn't defining God, but it was basically a list of what I thought God was, and His power. I found myself writing this:

1. Forgiving
2. Loving
3. Sense of Humor
4. Teacher
5. Listener
6. Honest
7. On Time
8. Mysterious
9. Challenges Me
10. Helps Others I Pray for
11. Accepting
12. Ever Changing

I believe in my heart that this is a great list. I truly feel God has those things and more. What this list did for me is it got me to see God in a different light. Page 133 of the Big Book, the top of the page says: "We are sure God wants us to be happy, joyous and free. We cannot subscribe to the belief that this life is a vale of tears, though it once was just that for many of us. But it is clear that we made our own misery. God didn't do it. Avoid then the deliberate manufacture of misery, but if trouble comes, cheerfully capitalize on it as an opportunity to demonstrate His omnipotence."

Now I had to look up what omnipotence meant—it basically means "power and authority." My current sponsor turned me on to that page and it's one I apply every day to my life.

I always looked at God as a punishing God who chastised me for my wrongs in life, one who would take people away from me in my life, because he hated me. Yet, I would pray to God, if I wanted out of a jam in my life. Ah, yes, the good ol' foxhole prayer. Then, as I would get through a difficult situation, I would think to myself, "Maybe I took that too far with the whole God thing." A good example of that would be when I got my DUI in 2012.

I was handcuffed in the back of a cop car on I-75 just a mile away from the exit to my house praying to God to get me out of this situation and I wouldn't drink again. Well, I went to jail, and when I got out, I lasted a couple of weeks sober. I knew I should probably stop, but I kept walking back on what I prayed to God about, because I didn't get my way.

As Bill W. says in his story in the *Big Book* on page 4, "As I drank, the old fierce determination to win came back." Also on page 31 of the *Big Book* in "More About Alcoholism," the first full paragraph says, "Despite all we can say, many who are real alcoholics are not going to believe they are in that class. By every form of self-deception and experimentation, they will try to prove themselves as exceptions to the rule, therefore nonalcoholic." Lastly on page 32 of the *Big Book,* first full paragraph, the second sentence says: "But the difficulty is that few alcoholics have enough desire to stop while there is yet time."

My insane thinking was the precursor to that first drink. My thoughts were: "Well, those cops had no business stopping me, because they were looking for trouble." Or, "If I just hadn't taken I-75 at 2 am, I would have been fine." Then thinking back to the prayer that I said to God in the cop car, my "I'm not going to drink anymore" turned into "Well, I'm just not going to drink and drive anymore." Right before I went to treatment in 2022, that was a promise that was long gone.

By the grace of God, I didn't get another DUI. How, I don't know.

I can relate to Bill. I drank of my thoughts first back then, and then after treatment in 2022. Back in 2012, it led to that old fierce determination to win by trying to control my drinking and drug using. After treatment in 2022, I was scared to drink and use again, but I was at the point where I had a body that couldn't process alcohol and a mind that couldn't process reality. The thought of relapse scared me back into meetings and catapulted this recovery journey. I had thoughts of still being able to control this disease. I was miserable.

Time is a funny thing. It's like the great alcoholic Achilles Heel. For my whole life I always thought time was on my side as far as seeing someone I hadn't seen in a while, getting sober, if I couldn't get sober that day, the next day would be my next attempt. Even in early recovery, I thought there would always be time to start the program of action. The truth is, today is all we have. This moment is all we have.

My current sponsor did a great job with me on this step. He didn't tell me I had to come to believe immediately, but what he did was show me with his actions was how God was working in *his* life. We spent hours talking about God. How God wants us to be happy, joyous, and free. We spent a ton of time talking about this list of attributes.

I started to believe, because I saw people in the fellowship believing. Then I believed more, because my sponsor believed so much in this idea of a God, who was so personal to him. He believed that this God understood and could move mountains, as long as he bought a shovel. Then it happened—I came to believe. This is the story of how I came to believe.

When I moved to Florida in 2006, I was on my road trip coming across I-10 from Alabama to Florida. As I was crossing a bridge into Florida, I looked out to the right. There were birds flying along the coastline. I had also seen oil rigs on that journey, and the sun was setting. On the radio was this song called *Hate Me* by a band called Blue October. It was my first time hearing this song—it's a beautiful song, but I took it as a very sad song. As I looked at the sunset, while crossing that bridge, it symbolized how I had always felt inside. The sun was always going down and there was an impending sense of doom.

Right before I entered this Step 2 business, I was in Ft. Lauderdale in the early morning, heading out to one of the islands. As I was crossing a drawbridge, I looked out the right and saw the coastline, lined with birds and cruise ships. It was a glorious sunrise, and that same song by Blue October was playing on the radio. In that moment, the rising sun expressed how I felt inside—hopeful and that everything was going to be OK. I felt as if something bigger than myself was truly looking out for me and had my best interests in mind.

The song, *Hate Me* by Blue October, was explained in a live performance by the singer, whom I watched during this time. It is an apology letter, and it changed my perspective on that song. It's kind of funny how God shows up. He is truly always on time, whether I see it or not. Now here is the third part to that story.

After I achieved my firsts year sober, I was living back in Sarasota for a few months. I was asked to come back to North Miami to do service and speak. As I was crossing Alligator Alley, I had the windows down in the car and the moon roof open, the wind was blowing, it was warm, and yet cool. I looked through the windshield up at the sky, which was a shade of bright blue I had never seen before in my life. Not a cloud in that brilliantly blue sky and that same Blue October song was playing on the radio, and I felt incredibly free. That feeling of freedom swept over me in a powerful blast and I couldn't stop smiling. I was really sure that God wanted me to be happy, joyous, and free.

The funny thing about *Step 2* is there is no timeline of when we come to believe and truly believe—it just happens. Sometimes with a little help from friends and sometimes from situations that God places in our lives. I came to believe that day on the bridge in Ft. Lauderdale. I came to see that page 133 in the *Big Book* is true, that day on Alligator Alley in June of 2023.

Yes, God is forgiving, loving, and he has a sense of humor. He is also a teacher, a wonderful listener, and He helps me stay honest. He's always on time and He is definitely mysterious, as He challenges me and helps others for whom I pray, He is accepting, but always ever-changing in his messages.

Last year the paper, with that list of attributes of my Higher Power on it, that I always kept close in my Big Book, fell out and disappeared. What didn't disappear was my belief in a Power greater than myself. I feel this was God's way of saying, "I am everything or I am nothing."

It's true. That God of my understanding is everything or nothing to me, and I hope he is as proud of his gift as I am proud of his gift to me.

Chapter Five

Step 3

Made a decision to turn our will and our lives over to the care of God as we understood him.

This was a huge step and a big decision for this alcoholic. When I worked with my first sponsor, the one in name only, I learned you can't transmit what you don't have. Now this statement isn't ripping on someone's sobriety and recovery, but I learned very quickly about the difference between sobriety and recovery.

He has the recovery that he has and that's fine for him. One day, my "sponsor in name only" and I went for lunch at Denny's to eat and to start working on the steps. He said something very interesting, "OK, open your *Big Book* and turn to the page with the steps."

I said, "OK, what page is that?" He told me to flip the pages until I found it.

Once I was on the right page, he asked me if I felt that I was powerless and that my life had become unmanageable. So I nodded and said, "Yes," without knowing what that meant.

Then he asked me if I believed that a power greater than myself could restore me to sanity, so I said, "Sure."

Then he asked me if I was willing to make a decision to turn my will and life over to my Lord and Savior, Jesus Christ. "Hold on," I said. "I don't think that's it."

That was my immediate thought, but then he insisted that I write down all my resentments and discuss them with him. I came to the decision right then and there that I was pretty much done with him. I never told him that we were done. I just let him figure it out for himself.

At that point in my recovery, I still wasn't at ease with the word, "God," let alone some religious Jesus. Not my jam, at all. I was walking around at the time with a huge resentment towards religion and God. Look, I firmly believe you can't transmit something you don't have. That may have been his recovery, but it wasn't at all the recovery I was seeking. Yes, it has worked for him for years, but there was no way that recovery, or whatever that was, would work for me. I knew it deep down.

When I worked this step with my current sponsor he took me to page 60 and 61 of the *Big Book*. He had me read the last paragraph on page 60 through the end of page 61 and, of course, we read "How It Works" before that. He made sure I was completely clear on the three pertinent ideas at the end of "How It Works" and yes, I was alcoholic and could not manage my own life. Yes, no human power could have relieved my alcoholism, and yes, God could and would, if He were sought.

Now I just had to start letting go of the idea that I was the director or a great general manager of the universe. On page 549 of the *Big Book,* in the personal stories, the author of *Freedom from Bondage* writes in the last paragraph, "They said if you want to know how this program works, take the first word of your question—the H is for honesty, the O is for open-mindedness, and the W is for willingness—these our *Big Book* calls the essentials of recovery."

I had to become willing and make a decision. If I was honest and opened my mind to this new idea that God was going to be my new director, then things might turn around for me.

On page 62 of the *Big Book*, the second full paragraph says, "So our troubles, we think, are basically of our own making. They arise out of one's self, and the alcoholic is an extreme example of self-will run riot, though he usually doesn't think so. Above everything, we alcoholics must be rid of selfishness. We must, or it kills us! God makes that possible and there often seems no way of entirely getting rid of self without His aid."

On Page 63 of the *Big Book,* the first full paragraph says, "When we sincerely took such a position, all sorts of remarkable things followed. We had a new Employer. Being all powerful, He provided what we needed, if we kept close to Him and performed His work well."

Now when I did the Third Step prayer with my sponsor, I didn't feel any different, but I did start letting go of my old ideas and ways—just some, a little at a time and started to work on them. I know that I had to stop controlling things as far as how my recovery went. I couldn't control who I was in recovery with, how a meeting went, or how the steps would start working in my life.

My sponsor told me that the only three things that I could control were my effort, my attitude, and my reaction. I had to stop trying to control the recovery process and just let go. I did this slowly, as I am not the director anymore, so it took a while. I'd like to share the story of when I completely let go the first time, and just simply let God start to work in my life.

I moved back to Sarasota in April of 2023 from Hollywood, Florida. I came back to be closer to my daughter, to make amends for certain financial things that I needed to make right in life, and to make amends to others whom I had wronged. After I was back for a while, I started to panic. I began questioning if I had made a mistake in coming back. I never wanted to come back to Sarasota permanently. It wasn't what I had planned in my recovery journey. I was in my head one day and decided that I needed a meeting immediately, so I looked up on my Meeting Guide app to find where a good one might be located.

I found this Sunset Beach Meeting on Holmes Beach. I packed up my foldable beach chair, grabbed my *Big Book,* and made the drive out there. When I arrived at Holmes Beach, I spotted the meeting, as the members of the fellowship were circled up out in the sand, all sitting in their chairs. I joined the circle and talked with others before the meeting.

The spot where they were circled up in was very interesting, as it was right next to some beach volleyball nets. In front of them was a beachside outdoor restaurant with a band playing and people drinking. Out near the water's edge were tons of people and families enjoying the evening.

When the meeting kicked off, we read aloud the readings and then read from pages 100-101 from the *Big Book*. I found it odd, because that is my favorite reading from the book. Then we proceeded to share around the circle. It was a very good meeting.

When the meeting was coming to a close, someone read the 9th Step Promises, and just as the last sentence was being read and the last word uttered, the sun immediately dipped below the horizon. All went quiet except for the distant noise of children playing and seagulls. The sky lit up with this brilliant bright orange color. Then, a warm breeze coming from the Gulf of Mexico followed. In that brilliant orange sky, that warm beach breeze gave me an overwhelming sense of peace. I knew at that moment that I was exactly where God wanted me to be.

For what purpose? I have zero idea, but I stopped wondering if it was his will or mine that I was back in Sarasota. God creates the greatest paintings, and He writes the best scripts. He is a virtuous employer and a great director. I can't do God's will my way or try to figure it out. I had to let go of trying to control the results. At that moment, I did.

Part of one of the personal stories in the *Big Book* is called, *The Man Who Mastered Fear* (on page 252). In the first full paragraph, this author talks about how he never wanted to see his hometown of Detroit again. However, then he realized it was the place where he could be of maximum service to God and AA.

A passage on page 253, in the second full paragraph, says, "I was supposed to be doing God's will, not mine. His road lay clear before me, and I'd better quit rationalizing myself into any detours." That is a great example of letting go and letting God. I almost talked myself into going back to Hollywood in fear of whatever lay before me in Sarasota. I now see that this is the place where I can be of maximum service and grow in understanding and effectiveness.

Chapter Six

Step 4

Made a searching and fearless
moral inventory of ourselves.

On page 64 of the *Big Book,* at the top of the page, it says something very interesting: "Our liquor was but a symptom. So we had to get down to causes and conditions."

For the longest time, this was the step of which I was most terrified. I knew all these things already that I was about to put on paper, but the fact that I had to actually look at myself was even scarier. My sponsor told me not to worry, as the fourth step would take about eight weeks to do—six weeks of that to procrastinate and two to actually do it. That still cracks me up when I think back to what he told me.

It's true though. I have heard people share in the rooms about how they are so scared of this step. Then I hear people share how they were scared, but after it was over, they wondered why they waited so long. Just putting these things that I have held onto for so long on a piece of paper was incredibly relieving. On page 66 of the *Big Book,* the first full paragraph states, "It is plain that a life which includes deep resentment leads only to futility and unhappiness. To the precise extent that we permit these, do we squander the hours that might be worthwhile. But with the alcoholic, whose hope is the maintenance and growth of a spiritual experience, this business of resentment is infinitely grave. We found that it is fatal. For when harboring such feelings we shut ourselves off from the sunlight of the Spirit."

Then in the following paragraph, it says this: "If we were to live, we had to be free of anger."

These statements made sense to me and I knew well of anger. It ruled every aspect of my life for as long as I could remember. It's how I dealt with situations and life. I couldn't handle not getting my way—when I didn't, I would get upset. Probably the most painful thing in recovery was knowing that I needed to take this step. However, I held off for so long, I was in great pain before actually starting the fourth step. Right before the time came for this step, I was begging my sponsor to put me into it. After starting this step, I felt like I was actually entering recovery.

In the *Big Book* on page 82, the third full paragraph says, "The alcoholic is like a tornado roaring his way through the lives of others. Hearts are broken. Sweet relationships are dead. Affections have been uprooted. Selfish and inconsiderate habits have kept the home in turmoil. We feel a man is unthinking when he says that sobriety is enough. He is like the farmer who came up out of his cyclone cellar to find his home ruined. To his wife, he remarked, "Don't see anything the matter here, Ma. Ain't it grand that the wind stopped blowin'?"

First off, I love that old-timey language. Second, on page 65 of the *Big Book,* I fully agree that Mr. Brown needs his ass kicked, but then again, this isn't about Mr. Brown or anyone else's inventory. This is about my personal inventory—a searching and fearless moral inventory of myself.

I would like to share some of my Step 4 with you, the Reader. If you are new in recovery, my hope is to show you there is nothing to be scared of. Fear is a wild emotion. It can grip you and not let go. The amazing part is the thing that lies on the other side of fear is bliss and it's priceless. The *Big Book* talks about fear and its effect on page 67, last paragraph. It says: "This short word somehow touches on every aspect of our lives. It was an evil and corroding thread;

the fabric of our existence was shot through with it. It set in motion trains of circumstances that brought us misfortune we felt we didn't deserve. But did not we, ourselves, set the ball rolling?"

Then on page 68 in the second paragraph, it talks about how we outgrow fear. It says, "Perhaps there is a better way—we think so. For now, we are on a different basis, the basis of trusting and relying upon God. We trust our infinite God rather than our finite selves. We are in the world to play the role He assigns. Just to the extent that we do as we think He would have us, and humbly rely on Him, does He enable us to match calamity with serenity."

This is the step where I had to trust my higher power completely to help me through. My sponsor wasn't going to put these things on paper for me and neither were any of my new friends in the fellowship. It works if I work it and God has my back. I remember when I wrote out this step, I invited God to sit with me while I did it. I think God likes to be invited into things in my life. That's my opinion though. So here is some of what I wrote with God's help.

My Mother

My mother and I hadn't spoken in twenty-two years at this point in my life. When I was a child, she and my dad divorced. I was two. I was sent to live with my dad's parents in the small town of Galva, Illinois. My mother lived in the same small town. I would see her out at the grocery store and run up to her to say hi. She would ignore me and not say hi, from what I remember. When I would see her driving down the road towards our car, I would become excited and wave like a child does, but she wouldn't wave back. I only saw her every few Christmas holidays. I tried to reconnect with her several times growing up, but we never really had a relationship.

After I came home from the Marine Corps in the year 2000, my cousin was having a high school graduation party and my mother was there. She looked terrible, almost like she was strung out on a crack binge. I cannot confirm that, but she was always a larger woman, yet now she was stick thin. She also had with her, my younger half-brother and half-sister, whom I had never met. At that party wherever I was, she didn't want to be. Now that I look back on it, maybe it was guilt and remorse for giving me up, but I'm not sure. Either way, she and I ended up getting into a verbal argument privately, when she raised a hand to hit me. I went full Drill Instructor on her and let her know exactly what I thought about her and the way she had treated me my whole life. I remember screaming in her face that I never wanted to see her or talk to her again. She took my two younger siblings and left the party. After that I never saw or talked to her again.

Page 551 of the *Big Book* in the story Freedom from Bondage talks about this exact resentment and says:

This resentment was against my mother, and it was twenty-five years old. I had fed it, fanned it, and nurtured it as one might a delicate child, until it had become as much a part of me as my breathing. It had provided me with excuses for my lack of education, my marital failures, personal failures, inadequacy, and of course, my alcoholism. And though I really thought I had been willing to part with it, now I knew I was reluctant to let it go."

This resentment affected everything in my life and still does somewhat, to this very day. Not as much as it used to be, but holding on to that resentment affected every relationship I was ever in. When a girl would break up with me in my younger years, out of nowhere I would wonder why she abandoned me. Then it hurt so much, when she gave her love and attention to another, especially if it was a friend of mine.

It changed my view of women. In my relationships, I would hurt them before they could hurt me. It became my greatest defense mechanism. In my first marriage, it was the cause of that relationship's destruction. Now with my first marriage, I can't shoulder all the blame, but it set the ball in motion for a glorious explosion at the end. It also played a part in my sexual behavior over the years and also in the downfall of my second marriage. I carried this resentment for twenty-two years and it was eating me alive. My role was simply holding on to this resentment as an excuse to womanize, drink, and use.

My sponsor asked if it served me anymore. I said it didn't, so we worked on throwing it into the trash. This was a tough one to let go of and was my biggest excuse for using and drinking. If I wanted to get better I had to swallow my pride, put my fragile ego aside, and let it go.

My Father

When I was young, my father ended up moving to Florida. My grandmother said it was so he could be OK. She told me growing up to never drink, because my dad was an alcoholic. I never knew what that meant. She never explained to me what that was. Over the years when I was growing up, my father would call on special days like holidays, and come to see me every few years. I always felt like that I was the last thing on his mind. Once again, this resentment grew from a young age.

I remember coming to Sarasota, Florida, to visit my dad when I was twelve and we did some things together, like Disney World and Busch Gardens. He even took me with him to an AA meeting. I don't remember anything about that meeting except that the cigarette smoke was so thick you could move it with your hand, and I could smell the coffee and hear the laughter. Then a few days later, I was back on a plane to go back to Illinois to my home with my grandparents. I was so sad to leave my dad. I remember crying the whole flight home. I missed my dad terribly.

In the late 90s, I came down to Florida to live with him, but I felt we never had a close relationship. Now I want to say this clearly. My dad did prepare me a room that he built onto the house. He did his best to make me feel at home, but I never felt secure or at home. I thought it was going to be a chance for us to grow closer. I was in my late teen years and he was going through things in life. I ended up getting kicked out of his house. I felt abandoned and thrown away *again*.

He was there for me on several occasions, but I never felt he was there for me the way a father should be there for a son. I never really heard him say, "I love you," or if he ever mentioned that he was happy that I was there. Some years passed and I had moved all over the country.

I ended up coming back to live with him without notice in 2006. He graciously took me in, but I moved out three months later. After I got my DUI in 2012, he tried to get me into Alcoholics Anonymous, but I was angry that I might end up like him and I didn't want to be an alcoholic.

An alcoholic abandons his kid and doesn't love his child. An alcoholic is an angry son of a bitch. These are the thoughts that I had at the time. An alcoholic has no fun in life. The *Big Book* talks about this thought. It's on page 393 in the story called, "The Perpetual Quest." In the first full paragraph it says, "When he told me he went to AA meetings three or four times a week, I thought, *Poor man, he has nothing better to do. What a boring life it must be for him, running around to AA meetings with nothing to drink!* Boring indeed—no bouncing off walls, no falling down stairs, no regular trips to the hospital emergency rooms, no lost cars, and on and on."

I didn't want to be like my old man. I watched him stay single, laying on the couch all the time, and doing nothing with his life. This was my perception. He also said he was a man of God. I never thought he was.

Sometime before 2016, my father was diagnosed with colon cancer. I went to the hospital and saw him before surgery. He said he loved me before he went in. I was so angry. I felt he only said this to make himself feel better. He had plenty of opportunities to say it many times before. Why now? He came out of surgery fine and was going to be OK. He got lucky—he had to use a colostomy bag and went through chemo. While he was doing that, the one and only time I really saw him was when he showed up at my house. He wanted me to sit with him while the medicine was giving him side effects.

I was so angry. In my head, he was there for his own selfish needs. He had plenty of opportunities to see me at any time. On Facebook, he would say nice things about me, but the resentment grew out of control. Why wouldn't he say it to my face? I felt like it was his excuse to look like a good father.

Then I saw him post about how some friends canceled dinner plans with him and so he wasn't going to go to dinner. That really caused this resentment to grow more, because why didn't he call me and ask to go to dinner?

In 2016 after the election, I found out who he voted for and I lost it on him. I called him up and told him that I never wanted to see him again and that he was never going to see his granddaughter again, because of the way he voted. I also told him that I hoped his cancer would come back and he would just die. After that explosion, my drinking and drug use exploded in return.

My dad and I didn't talk for five years. Now looking back at it, my intolerance, my inability to accept him for who he was, and my intolerance towards his political views cost us five years of our lives together. My anger cost me and my daughter five years of any time left with him. In those five years, my father's cancer came back, and he had other issues hit him.

Right before I went to treatment, I messaged him to apologize and invite him back into our lives. The guilt was tearing me up. I knew deep in my heart I wasn't this person who says things like I did five years prior. We reconnected and ended up going to dinner. The only problem was, I was in full-blown addiction and out of my mind high at dinner. That was the last time we saw each other until I was in recovery.

Now in recovery, we reconnected, but not till after my fourth step. My sponsor encouraged me to let go of this resentment due to its heavy nature. It ate at my soul. Deep down I know I am a loving man who cares about others and their views. That is why now, in my recovery, I don't talk politics with anyone. Political differences cost me five years with my father. It still bothers me to this day when I see people fighting about politics. Those views rip families and friends apart. It's a subject that is hard to practice with love and tolerance—especially acceptance. I choose now not to get involved with anyone in this delicate area. I now respect people's views, no matter what they are.

However, there were other ridiculous resentments in my fourth step—things like big box stores. This resentment is an interesting one, so let me dive into it. Maybe you can relate or identify.

In my woodworking career, I had to make frequent trips to my local big box hardware store for supplies. I couldn't accept the fact that service in stores like this has gone downhill a bit. I remember the days when you could walk into a store and employees were helpful. If I needed something from the plumbing section, there was someone knowledgeable in that section. I didn't feel like this was the case anymore. So when the automatic doors to the store would open and I'd walk in, Mark would stay outside, while my "Inner Dictator" would be the one doing the shopping. Some of us know that persona very well.

It's the one that acts like, "WHERE ARE ALL OF MY SERVANTS?" The one that wonders, "WHY HAVEN'T THE EMPLOYEES IN THIS STORE ROLLED OUT MY RED CARPET YET?" The one that yells, "WHAT DO YOU MEAN THAT"S NOT IN STOCK? BRING ME YOUR MANAGER!" The one that makes sure YOU know, "DON'T YOU KNOW WHO I AM?"

My sponsor laughed at that resentment and spoke to me in great lengths about my sense of entitlement. That sense would even come out in restaurants, too. Now I would never mess with the person handling my food. It's the golden rule of the restaurant industry. I was a server for years and you are playing with fire, if you mess with your server before you get your food. BUT, here was my attitude in restaurants.

"WHY IS THE MUSIC THIS LOUD?" Then I would go on to explain to my date or whoever was with me that when I used to be a restaurant manager, I would have never allowed the music to play at this volume, because it makes for an unsatisfactory guest experience. Or I might say to my date or whoever was with me, "WHY IS THE SERVICE SO SLOW? Back when I was a server, I was taught to give better service and to take care of my tables! Who trains their staff to be so inattentive and slow?"

Yup, that was my sense of entitlement for a lot of years and even so, to some degree in my early recovery. My sponsor asked me if that resentment and sense of entitlement served me anymore. My answer was a clear-cut, "No." Acting that way didn't bring me happiness and definitely didn't bring anyone else happiness either. It was imperative that I worked on it immediately.

He explained in detail that we never know what someone may be going through in their life. They may be having a hard day or they could have had to work, even though they're sick. They could have just lost someone in their life and might not be completely focused that day. They could even have a sick relative whom they are worried about and the list goes on from there.

My first-world problems might not mean that much compared to their real-world problems. He started to teach me that kindness was the way of life that was the most spiritually rewarding. This made total sense, because my sponsor showed this to me in his interactions with others daily. I saw this first-hand regularly.

He also let me know that God likes to show up and see firsthand how we are living. He might be that person working in the store or serving that table. He could even be the customer standing behind me or the restaurant guest sitting in the booth next to me. My sponsor's explanation of this made complete sense to me.

I had the police on my list of resentments, because they gave a nice guy like me, who was minding his own business, a DUI.

The dopeman was on my list, because he took advantage of me. Even though he never held a gun to my head one single time and demanded, "USE THOSE DRUGS RIGHT NOW!" That one is a delicate resentment, because it's crazy of me to think that particular resentment was all my fault. He did take advantage of my addiction for his gain, but once again he never forced me to use drugs. I love gray areas in recovery. Isn't that what a dopeman does? You know, make money feeding my addiction? That's the business he is in.

My aunt and uncle on my dad's side of the family were on the list. I HATED my aunt. I felt she treated me like I was "less than" most of my life, judged me, and looked at me like I was the black sheep of the family. She even told me that I *was* the black sheep one time. I looked up to her as a child and she was my favorite aunt—not anymore. It hurt how I felt when she looked at me and her ideas about my direction and life. Now her and my uncle did invite me to live with them in my senior year of high school and they did the best with me that they could. They did want the best for me, but I just didn't feel like the direction they wanted me to take was the best one for me.

I was so resentful at her after she made me move out at eighteen that I spent the whole summer after high school tripping on LSD. That summer was also when I tried meth and cocaine for the first time. Of course LSD was way more fun, so I just stuck with that for the summer. As I look back now, I was never really taught responsibility and maybe—just maybe—that's what they were trying to do.

Today I think she is all right and that my uncle is a pretty amazing guy. I was just an angry teenager who was mad at the world. That resentment didn't serve me or anyone. It was just another excuse to drink and use drugs so, of course, I had to throw it in the trash.

My current ex-wife was on the list, My first ex-wife was on there, also, because she left me for her best friend's dad. She was 20 and he was in his 40s. I never let that one go. It was a great excuse to use drugs and drink. It wasn't all my fault but I still used it as a reason to drown my sorrows into oblivion. The list goes on from there, but the thing that interested me the most was my fears list. One of my biggest fears was this: the fear of, "What will people think?" Let me explain that one.

Growing up, I was bullied heavily in junior high and high school. I had to learn martial arts to defend myself. I would walk down the halls of my small high school and get hit out of nowhere—kicked, punched, and slammed into lockers. I would be called faggot, queer, homo, ugly, and more. I would be told I was worthless and would never amount to anything. I had close to no friends and the ones I had were so-called outcasts.

Now, I held on to this resentment for a long time, but let me give you, the Reader, a look into the mental twist that comes from being bullied. It stole my self-confidence in life and made me second-guess everything. My self-esteem, for the most part, has been low since then, and affects my relationships and more. When I would try to date someone as a teenager, they would say how ugly my girlfriend was and how I could never do better, and lots more. It made me feel less than others for most of my life. It made me fear being trapped by anything or in any situation.

To this day, I hate feeling cornered. That feeling has gotten better, but it's not completely gone and I'm not so sure it ever leaves. It affects me ever feeling safe and secure. I've had to really work hard to overcome that feeling of never being safe. To this day, it sometimes does come up, but it's less severe than it was for many, many years. It has helped to fuel my fear of "what will people think." That fear has kept me from achieving so much in my life.

After I became successful in my life and things fell apart, I thought these people from high school had been waiting to witness my downfall so my use spiraled out of control from fear. I couldn't let them ever see me fail, so that is what fueled the start of the business. I had to become so successful—they would eat their words. It fueled the wrong intent in a lot of my affairs. I always felt when someone would laugh and look in my direction that they were making fun of me and talking about me. It stopped me from getting sober sooner and to admit that I had a drug and alcohol issue. It was my hardest fear to overcome. It fueled the "fear of the unknown," and many other fears. It still lingers to some extent, but not as heavy now. It's close to almost non-existent.

On pages 255-256 of the *Big Book* in the story called, "The Man Who Mastered Fear," it talks about this. The last paragraph says, "It would be wonderful were I able to tell you that my confidence in God and my application of the Twelve Steps to my daily living have utterly banished fear. But this would not be the truth. The most accurate answer I can give you is this: Fear has never again ruled my life since that day in September 1938, when I found that a Power greater than myself could not only restore me to sanity, but could keep me both sober and sane. Never in sixteen years have I dodged anything because I was afraid of it. I have faced life instead of running away from it."

I get up every day and do my best to grow further apart from this fear and the other ones that gripped my life for so long. I am not perfect and sometimes, they come up in certain situations. I'll talk about that later towards the end of this book, but the point is that I am better now at facing them. That doesn't mean it is easy to do so, but this means I've been able to cope better and trust in God. Speaking of this amazing God of my understanding, let's move on to the next subject.

Chapter Seven

Step 5

Admitted to God, to ourselves, and to another human being the exact nature of our wrongs.

OK, let's get something straight before I rip into this story. Now that I look back at things, this was the step that I was the most terrified of—not Step 4. This is where my fear of, "What will people think?" comes into play. You mean to tell me that I have to sit down with someone and tell them the things I have done? The short answer is, "Yes." As a newcomer, this was overwhelming to me. This step takes a lot of courage.

In the *Big Book,* there are several passages that explain why this is such a vital step. On page 73 first full paragraph it says, "More than most people, the alcoholic leads a double life. He is very much the actor. To the outer world he presents his stage character. This is the one he likes his fellows to see. He wants to enjoy a certain reputation, but knows in his heart he doesn't deserve it. The inconsistency is made worse by the things he does on his sprees. Coming to his senses, he is revolted at certain episodes he vaguely remembers. These memories are a nightmare. He trembles to think one might have observed him. As fast as he can, he pushes these memories far inside himself. He hopes they will never see the light of day. He is under constant fear and tension—that makes for more drinking."

On page 72 of the *Big Book* in the second full paragraph about the seventh sentence down, it states: "If we skip this vital step, we may not overcome drinking. Time after time newcomers have tried to keep to themselves certain facts about their lives. Trying to avoid this humbling experience, they have turned to easier methods. Almost invariably they got drunk."

Myself, I relate these two passages to two specific pages and lines in the *Big Book*. On page 88, in the last paragraph it says, "We alcoholics are undisciplined." Also on page 204 in the story, "Women Suffer Too," right before the last paragraph, there is a line that says, "Inwardly frightened, outwardly defiant."

These lines explain so much in so few words. For a large portion of my life, I have never had the guts to follow through with anything. I've always put on a tough face on the outside, but resisted change at every turn, due to being truly terrified inside. Now the steps once again have made that easier to deal with, but it does still linger in certain situations. The *Big Book* doesn't say I have to do this vital step with a sponsor and in fact, it gives many examples of people with whom I may do it. It does however lay out a couple of disclaimers on page 74 at the end of the first paragraph into the first full paragraph. It says: "Of course, we sometimes encounter people who do not understand alcoholics. If we cannot or would rather not do this, we search our acquaintance for a close-mouthed, understanding friend."

I can closely relate these passages to one more thing. On page xxviii of the "Doctor's Opinion," it specifically says, "Frothy emotional appeal seldom suffices. The message which can interest and hold these alcoholic people must have depth and weight."

Look, it took an alcoholic to reach into my soul and pull my head out of my butt. Plain and simple. I have tried therapy for years and have tried to talk to other people about my addictions. I have felt like an alcoholic understands me better than many others have. I am more swayed to talk to an alcoholic who understands about my past indiscretions. They just get it. Usually nine times out of ten, an alcoholic won't be shocked about the things I have done or gone through, because they have done the same, worse, or can relate.

Now I have done a mini fifth step with my recent girlfriend about a thing from my past that I felt she needed to know, because yes, it could affect our relationship moving forward. Before I told her about these things, I read to her from the *Big Book* and explained why it was important. I read from page 75 to help her understand better. It was eating me up and as she listened, she was tight-lipped. I respect her for that. I know even though she isn't like me, I could trust her with this secret from the past. It was going to cause me to drink due to the turmoil of holding it back from her. I care that deeply for her and it was that important she knew. It actually brought us closer together and to this day, I love her more because of her kind heart and understanding.

Now, I had that same secret out when I worked the fifth step with my sponsor, but I have never been that open with a woman ever, till that point. It was liberating, she understood, and we moved forward. To this very day though I am very tight-lipped about things in my life with other people, because yes there are people in this world who do not understand the alcoholic, and will judge, give unsolicited viewpoints, and advice. I'm very careful with whom I open up to and keep in my life.

When it came time to sit down with my sponsor to do this step, I was hesitant and scared. He reassured me I had nothing to worry about. We went to a park that was quiet and private. It was his special spot to do the fifth step. We prayed beforehand and he listened. He even told me some things he had done in his past and it helped dissolve the fears about doing this step. I love my sponsor. He is a caring man who is very understanding and nonjudgmental. He helped me feel comfortable and OK. Besides, he is an alcoholic. He has zero reason to judge anyone.

When we came to the end of the step, I asked him what he thought. He let out a deep sigh, laughed for a second, and said that he definitely thought I was selfish and self-centered. When he said that, my mind said in return, "Would the results have been different had I left out a couple of things?" Now that I think back on that day and that thought, I laugh. I guess I am truly an alcoholic.

In Danny Falcone's book, *The 20 Most Misunderstood, Misinterpreted, Mistakes of the Big Book of Alcoholics Anonymous*, he explains the reason for this step very clearly. On page 79 of his book he says this, "Have you ever wondered why we admit these things to God, to ourselves, and to another human being? We admit to God for forgiveness, to ourselves for understanding, and to another human being for humility."

I'm so happy I did this vital step and conquered my fears with it. It has made me more of an open person and not so closed off. It has made me more trusting and has given me confidence to face my fears head on. Now that I understand its importance, I recommend it to anyone who is trying to recover from alcoholism.

Chapter Eight

Step 6 & 7

Were entirely ready to have God remove all these defects of character.

Humbly asked Him to remove our shortcomings.

When I first saw Step 6, I had zero idea what defects of character were. In fact, in my newcomer mind I thought, "Well, good thing I don't have any of those issues, so I can just skip those steps!" The truth is, I am riddled with them to my very core. I've spent my whole adult life living in those defects and showing them off proudly.

On page 65 of the book, *The Twelve and Twelve,* in the first full paragraph it says, "Since most of us are born with an abundance of natural desires, it isn't strange that we often let these far exceed their intended purpose. When they drive us blindly, or we willfully demand that they supply us with more satisfactions or pleasures than are possible or due us, that is the point at which we depart from the degree of perfection that God wishes for us here on earth. That is the measure of our character defects, or if you wish, of our sins."

I never understood, "defects of character," until I really buckled down and worked with my sponsor. The first thing he had me do was write out the definition of the PAGGLES on a piece of paper. What I ended up doing also was writing those definitions on the back cover of my *Big Book,* also. I still laugh today about this, because my first *Big Book* fell completely apart from overuse after the first year. When the back cover finally fell off, I asked my sponsor if that meant I was finally defect free. He laughed and shook his head no.

With the definition of Pride, Anger, Greed, Gluttony, Lust, Envy, and Sloth at my fingertips, I made my humble beginning through working and living Steps 6 and 7 in my life. After I had the definitions down and began to start seeing them, my sponsor handed me several sheets of paper. Those sheets of paper were weekly checklists of several defects of character—probably two dozen different defects of character and about a dozen assets of character at the bottom. At the top of the page was a checklist for each day of the week.

I cringed at this exercise. He had me carry a list with me every day in my pocket everywhere I went at any time. At the end of the week, we would look it over. I couldn't get around not doing it either. We saw each other just about every day, because we went to the same clubhouse daily for meetings. He was the type who would spontaneously ask me to see the list.

Now I had seen him work with others and if he gave them a task or homework as we call it, and they didn't have it with them and or it wasn't done, he would just give them a *look.* He never got on them, but the look was enough to have you feel like you really weren't doing the work. I never didn't do something he asked, because that look of disapproval was something I didn't want to experience firsthand.

Now this exercise isn't something that is suggested in the *Big Book* or any other AA-approved literature, but, hey, I was a tough case and he had a tough job with me. I like his technique so much, because he goes above and beyond to hand out strong recovery to people with whom he works. What this list ended up doing for me was help me realize each day I had different patterns and I also worked different assets to overcome those defects.

That list got me focusing more on my assets than my defects. It made me see that I'm not perfect by any means and gave me an awareness to a certain degree. In fact, the first time I handed him that list back after that first week, it was covered with gluttony. It had chip stains, coffee stains, food stains, and more on it.

Now after some time, we ended up doing the 7th Step prayer. We got down on our knees in the middle of the Stirling Room and let it rip. After the prayer, I opened my eyes, and nothing felt different. I wasn't levitating, I wasn't even glowing or pure. What I just did though, was invite God into my life to help me change my behaviors.

I'd like to share with you, the Reader, some great examples from books I've found that explain defects of character best to me.

In the book called *Drop the Rock* on page xv, in the introduction, in the first full paragraph it says, "Shoemaker wrote about the necessity of making daily surrenders. Yes, the Sixth Step is also about surrendering, just like the Third. But Shoemaker made one point very clear: We surrender as much of ourselves to as much of God as we understand. In other words, our spiritual progress is based in direct proportion to our dropping the rock. We are very fortunate that all of our defects aren't revealed to us all at once. Recovery works by giving us daily insight into what we can do to remove what blocks us. We need daily awareness that our character defects are the opposite of the principles of our program."

Two paragraphs down on that same page it says, "By working the Sixth and Seventh Steps, we are less likely in recovery to stay stuck in old, unproductive, negative behavior patterns."

Next on page xix of the Introduction in *Drop the Rock* it says, "To become the person we can become, we must drop the rock, all the grasping and holding on to old patterns of behaving, thinking, and feeling that are harmful to ourselves and to others."

There are many more things in *Drop the Rock* that hit me deep in my gut, but the big one is a simple line on page 4 in the second full paragraph. It says, "I cannot open a flower with a sledgehammer—only God opens flowers." Isn't that the truth! That line hits hard.

In the Danny Falcone book, *The 20 Most Misunderstood, Misinterpreted, Mistakes of the Big Book of Alcoholics Anonymous*, he says a couple of powerful things. On page 84 at the end of the next to the last paragraph he says, "God doesn't remove defects of character. He allows them to be replaced with something better if we put forth the effort." Then on page 85, in the first full paragraph he says, "Showing God that we are ready to change by what we do rather than words we say is a huge step for us." Last, but not least, if I go back a couple of pages to page 83, in the fourth paragraph he says, "But the change we're talking about here is not about what we get. It's about what we are willing to let go of. You can't take what God's trying to give you because your hands are full. You've got to let go of what you have in order to get something new."

All that knowledge is such a powerful tool in the battle against my defects of character. All those statements are true. I heard in a meeting once from an alcoholic that a leopard can't change its spots. True, but an alcoholic can change their ways, if they are really truly willing and ready. I've had to change *so* much behavior and it hasn't been easy. I'd like to share a story that directly relates to my Steps 6 and 7 experiences.

A couple of months after I left treatment, I was given an incredible career opportunity with a company in Ft. Lauderdale called Interior Systems Manufacturing (ISM). They did what's called mega yacht refitting. I've been a woodworker since 2011 and they did the highest end of woodworking possible on multi-million dollar mega yachts. When I applied for this job, I had no idea what I was getting into. When I saw the ad on the Indeed website, all it really said was, "Do you like a challenge?"

I thought to myself, "Of course I do." I really did—I just got sober, so there is that. Now by this time in my life, I had an extensive portfolio of work from over the past years and my skill level was through the roof. My portfolio got me the job, but when they told me what they actually did, I was intimidated. The owner of the company offered me an incredible salary and told me that they were going to teach me new techniques from the ground up. He also told me I would be working with the best of the best in the industry. This was mind-blowing, considering I had thought in treatment that my career was over and I didn't even know if I wanted to continue it.

However, God had different ideas. I took the offer, because I would be crazy to turn it down. I started and had to earn my spot. I learned new techniques and got to know the small crew of craftsmen. It was like a family and I quickly took to this new career. It was wild and became a part of me. It was in my blood and I was hooked from the first time I stepped onto a mega yacht. There was something ritualistic about packing out tools in the morning to go work on one of these awesome boats.

Loading what we made and our tools and pulling into the boatyard, before going on to the boat as a team, and being in the middle of the action. I would put my headphones on for the ride over in the van, and get pumped up to do my best every day. I loved being in the shop. It was high-end and professional. I learned so much from the craftsman already working there and from the owner, Winfield. I can't thank him enough for helping me get my wheels back under me, and for taking a chance on a woodworker who was in recovery. I didn't hide my recovery from him either. It was important he knew, because I was new to recovery. If I had to call my sponsor or another alcoholic if I were to become overwhelmed, he deserves the right to know why I would be on the phone. I had a lot of respect for him and I did my best for him every day.

I remember the first time he said that he trusted me. That was huge for me. To hear the words, "I trust you," was empowering. Do you know how long it had been since I heard those words from anyone? I immediately called a friend of mine in the program and she was so excited that he said those words to me! She and I laughed and then she said, "That's great! The first time I heard that, I felt like I had just won an Oscar!" We laughed and it was the best day.

Some time passed at the shop, as I earned my workbench and workstation. I had to arrange everything from the ground up, but I took a lot of pride in it. I set my station up not only to look good, but I also tricked it out with a mini fridge and a coffee pot. I even set up cups with a bunch of different sweeteners, sugar, and creamers. Every morning I brewed a couple pots of coffee. I was surprised nobody had made coffee in the mornings there before.

I had become a coffee connoisseur of sorts in my recovery. I loved a finely aged 5:30 pm coffee at the 8:30 Stirling Room meetings. The West Dixie Club in North Miami had the best cup at the 9:30 Breakfast Club meetings. I remember opening the doors to the club and smelling that sweet pot of God beans. My favorite was a vintage 2022 Folgers. I noticed that I drank my coffee like an alcoholic. I drank it because I was thirsty and the more I drank, the thirstier I got. I also noticed that I would drink three quarters of the cup and let the last quarter cool enough to do it like a shot. I still laugh about coming to realize that. It took another alcoholic to point that one out to me. Thank you, God.

So, anyway, a strange thing happened after I started to make coffee. Every morning, a couple of the guys started hanging out around my bench and fellowshipped. Then a few more came along day after day. The next thing I knew, every day my bench became the place to be. I loved it. They asked if they could pitch in some money and I turned them down. The joy of the camaraderie and unity was payment enough. When I got to know these guys more, it reminded me of the rooms. How many times had I met someone new over a cup of coffee that started with a simple hello and a handshake? Those moments sparked unity and the momentum to get to know new people on a deeper level.

A week or so goes by with those morning gatherings at my workstation, when this guy comes over. He asked if I wanted to go to lunch later that day. Now this guy wasn't really liked. He was standoffish to others and they were the same with him. When he came over and asked me, my first thought was "Oh great! This guy." I had a preconceived notion of him due to how others talked about him. I reluctantly said yes and he said he would ride with me. I whipped out the Set Aside Prayer before we went to lunch along with the Serenity Prayer.

We left and went to my favorite spot near the shop called Lester's Diner. Turns out, he loved Lester's Diner, too. I was hooked on this diner, because a lot of people in recovery go there to eat after the meetings. Quite a few other folks in recovery work there, too.

We went in and sat down. I was hesitant to have any meaningful conversation with him, but he started to change my perspective quickly. I always ordered eggs, bacon, hash browns, and white toast. He insisted I try something different—he told me with confidence that I was missing out, if I didn't order the lamb chops. I hesitantly agreed and ordered. I can't lie. It was the finest meal I had ever had there. It filled me with joy, but the greatest part was that he and I had the best conversation.

He told me that he respected my work at the shop and the attention to detail that I put into things. That was amazing to hear, because I respected his work, too. He told me how much he liked my workstation. That felt good, because I put my heart and soul into that workstation.

Then, he started to tell me his story. He was from Venezuela and he came here to work to give himself and his family in his home country a better life. He said he was able to buy farmland there and he could live like, as he called it, "Mafioso." He showed me the great life he lived in his home country, because of the opportunities here. The pictures were fun to check out, as his face lit up. I could hear the gratitude in his voice. His eyes also shone as he talked about it. You know what? I couldn't find one reason to dislike him. I tried, but I couldn't find one.

We paid for lunch and went back to the shop, but we also had an enjoyable ride back. Every week from there on out, we went to lunch at least twice a week. Each time, he would get a big smile on his face and suggest a place that I had never heard of. I was able to experience culture like no other. I ate real Jamaican food for the first time from a place that was located off the beaten path. I had some amazing barbeque at a restaurant that I would have never tried, if it hadn't been for him. We became friends and he even brought me coffee from his home country.

I ended up talking to another guy in the shop some time later. He told me that he liked the guy with whom I kept going to lunch. He also knew why this guy was standoffish to others, but he said he didn't give people his time, if they wouldn't give him theirs. That made sense. He didn't have to put his energy into making others like him.

When I moved back to Sarasota, I walked away from that company with a newfound respect for others around me—just by practicing the opposite of some of my defects of character. Sometimes people are just looking for others to be nice to them. Once again, a great conversation and friendship was formed over a cup of coffee. Thank you, God.

Chapter Nine

The Big Book Breakdown with William D. Jessworth MD, aka Doc

So this is the point of my book where I'm going to take a break from personally working with the steps and share a story about my experience with learning the *Big Book* from my sponsee, brother Doc. It's important because Doc and I became friends right around the time I started working the Sixth and Seventh Steps in my recovery. Let me start by sharing with you how I came to acquire my *Big Book*.

When I was in treatment, they used to load us up in the vans, aka the "Druggy Buggies," and take us to meetings nightly. I didn't really care for the meetings, except for one I really liked called "Bikers in Recovery." It was at a clubhouse in Hollywood, Florida, and still is an ongoing meeting to this day.

Those bikers LOVED recovery. They were loud and rowdy—the definition of happy, joyous, and free. They used to shout at each other during the readings at the start of the meeting. "How It Works" would get read and during the part that says, "Many of us exclaimed, 'What an order, I can't go through with it!' " and they would shout out things like "BULLSHIT! GET A SPONSOR!" "CALL YOUR SPONSOR!" or "CALL GOD!!!!!" They would even shout the step numbers out as they were read.

Any Lengths

Page 132 of the *Big Book,* first full paragraph says, "We have been speaking to you of serious, sometimes tragic things. We have been dealing with alcohol in its worst aspect. But we aren't a glum lot. If newcomers could see no joy or fun in our existence, they wouldn't want it. We absolutely insist on enjoying life." They were not a glum lot at all. After they were done shouting at each other during the readings, the chairperson would ring the bell and say, "It's time now to get serious," and they did.

When newcomers would share, they would smile and encourage them. They introduced themselves to newcomers afterwards, and encouraged us to keep coming back. At the end of every Bikers in Recovery meeting , they would do two things. They would have a raffle for a shirt and a bumper sticker and they would give out a free *Big Book* to anyone who needed it.

There was a guy at that meeting every time, every week, who would hold up the book and shout out, "I'VE GOT A FREE *BIG BOOK* HERE FOR ANYONE THAT WANTS IT!" If nobody would jump at it, he would bait us by shouting out, "IT'S GOT PICTURES!" He got me with that one—I love pictures. I was so thrilled to maybe see some old-timey pics of Bill W. and Dr. Bob.

After I took the bait, I brought my new book back to the residential quarters at treatment and opened it. There were no pictures. (I still have a bone to pick with that guy today for baiting me.) So I did what anyone in early recovery with half a brain would do—I put it into a box I had in the corner of my room. And there it sat until I got serious about AA.

Hey! I had recovery in my life with that book near me, tucked away in a safe place. I laugh now at my ignorance in early recovery. Since I have become heavily invested in the *Big Book,* I can't imagine my recovery without its knowledge. It's become an extension of me. It goes with me everywhere. It is either next to me in bed when I wake up or on the nightstand. It goes with me to work and sits on my workbench. It always rides with me in my car. It's with me at every meeting.

In fact, I'm on my second one now, because my first one fell completely apart after only a year and a half. The cover had fallen off, it had no binding, and all the pages were heavily worn. They were not highlighted, but there were pen notes and underlines on every page. It had coffee and food stains on it and it was tinted a nice yellow color due to the smoke in the Stirling Room while it was still a smoking room. (They aren't anymore, since they moved locations.)

I said I would read that Big Book till the Doctor didn't have an opinion anymore. Well, he doesn't have an opinion anymore, as those pages have all fallen out. So what I did was I saved it and put it into a clear wall mounted display case. I can open it anytime to pull it out. Sometimes I carry it to meetings—I do that at treatment facilities to show newcomers how I did it. Funny thing is, the guy that shouted out about it having pictures was right. It does have pictures!

There are pictures of my first year and a half of recovery—all the meetings I chaired and I shared from it while speaking. It has the picture of me taking it up to the front of the West Dixie Club when I picked up my one year's medallion, so I could share a passage from a story that describes what AA means to me. I shared from page 509, the second full paragraph to the end of page 511 in the story, "Gutter Bravado." If you want a good read, check those pages out. I've even read from it when I've handed someone else *their* medallion.

It has pictures of the endless hours I spent with my current sponsor and others at the meetings in between meetings—reading, learning, talking, and laughing. It has pictures of family and friendship in it. I'll cherish those pictures always. The ones I will value the most though are of my dear friend, Volunteer Alex, to whom this book is dedicated and my dear friend, Jess aka Doc. I'll speak about Volunteer Alex later when it's time. This is about Doc right now.

Jess (or Doc) was a man I met at the Stirling Room, who is about my age. We talked casually for a few months, but never anymore interaction than that, but then I found out something interesting. We were sponsee brothers. He has more time than me and I noticed he was into the *Big Book* heavily. When we ended up connecting, he informed me he wasn't a *Big Book* "thumper." He was a *Big Book* "junkie"—interesting.

He proceeded to show me some things. He asked if I knew the book well and understood what it was talking about. I said, "No." That was the truth. I didn't comprehend what the stories were trying to say. Bill's story was coming out as "WAR FEVER" ran high in the New England birdman, boat thingy—two periods—"SUN and EAGLE." It was hieroglyphics to me. Plus, growing up, I could never read well, as words seem to scramble on pages—the only things I've ever really excelled at was art, band, and math. I love numbers and math—that intrigues me.

Jess looked at me and asked if I liked to take people's inventory. As it just so happens, I LOVED to take people's inventory. So we sat down together at the meeting between meetings at the Stirling Room and went through Bill's story. He said we were going to look for the disease progression, the PAGGLES, and defects of character. We took Bill's inventory up and down. When we would stumble on those things, he would say, "OK, let's turn to page so and so and check out the reference."

Then slowly something started to happen. I began to understand the *Big Book* from a mathematical point of view, so it started to actually stick and I began understanding what it was really saying. My reading became easier and I soaked it up like a sponge. Every day for weeks, we did that at the meeting before the meeting and the meetings after the meetings. We had a great room with the Stirling Room. They were open from 7am to 12am daily so when people sat around in between the meetings, they sat around at dining tables like family.

Jess and I became thick as thieves. We spent hours upon hours breaking the book down. My sponsor sat in, while others sat in as we were doing it and going deeper. My knowledge and knowing where things were and how they related to things shot through the roof.

One day, while Jess and I were breaking down the *Big Book* and a story or two, I looked at him and he looked at me. Then I said, "You know what?"

He asked, "What?"

I said, "You're pretty smart with this. I'm gonna start calling you William D. Jessworth, MD!"

He laughed and said, "What, like Dr. Silkworth from the 'Doctor's Opinion'?" I laughed and said, "Yup!"

He laughed and said, "Doc" and it stuck.

We started a meeting at the Stirling Room on Tuesday nights called "The *Big Book* Breakdown" and many showed up for recovery. That meeting was full of interaction and people coming up with their own references, while we broke down stories. Knowledge and references were flying around that room during that meeting and a good time was had by all.

Eventually my time came to an end in Hollywood, as I had to move back to Sarasota, but I'll never forget Doc. I owe my love of the *Big Book* and my knowledge about it to him. I have a feeling God put him in my life for a reason. He taught me how things tie together in the book and in the stories. He taught me how if I could relate my personal experiences with their personal experiences it now becomes a spiritual experience.

He showed me that the *Big Book* is way deeper than some make it out to be and there is a mathematical link to it all. I love how Bill W. wrote his story. I've noticed a lot of downplay about his run, but isn't that the alcoholic nature. It's like—really, Bill? How disturbed was Lois?

Whenever my sponsor, Doc, and I get together, we read and laugh. I see Doc from time to time when I travel over to the room I love so much. When we see each other, it's a great reunion. We pick up with the book like we never stopped. Also, I noticed something funny about our time together. At no time, while we were sitting at the Stirling Room, breaking down that book, forgetting about time altogether, did we drink or drug.

I saw Doc right before I wrote this chapter and asked him if it was OK if I wrote this about us. He had a huge smile on his face and said, "Of course!" I showed him my new *Big Book* that I'm breaking down now—it's already starting to get worn out after only three months and all the fresh things I found and new references. He was happy and joined in. I have made a friend for life and I can't thank him enough. I care if he lives or dies and I know he feels the same about me. We became more than friends. We became brothers—I've never had a real brother, but I consider him one.

Chapter Ten

Steps 8 & 9

Made a list of all persons we had harmed and became willing to make amends to them all.

Made direct amends to such people wherever possible, except when to do so would injure them or others.

To be completely honest I don't know if Step 8 or Step 9 ever really bothered me when I first looked at them with my sponsor. In fact, by the time I had gotten to them, I was actually excited to start cleaning up past things that I had done in life. When I was in treatment, I believe I fell victim to what most newcomers do—I wanted to immediately shout from the rooftops that I was finally sober and sorry for the wrongs I had done.

Now when I look back on it, how many times did I say in my life that I was sorry for behavior I was still doing. In the Danny Falcone book, *The 20 Most Misunderstood, Misinterpreted, Mistakes of the Big Book of Alcoholics Anonymous*, he states it best on page 94, first full paragraph. He lays it out very clearly in one sentence: "Do not make amends if you haven't quit doing the behavior."

I wondered in treatment why my wife at the time was still mad at me, even though I was getting sober. I wondered why my daughter wanted me to keep my distance. Why would old coworkers still be upset at me now that I had just gotten sober? I've learned that in this program of recovery, time takes time. I've had to learn that the hard way, through patience and total acceptance of any and all situations.

When I reached Step 8, my sponsor was very straightforward. I had become willing to make amends, so he had me make a list of all persons I had harmed using my Fourth Step list and adding others onto that list that I necessarily didn't have on my Step 4. When I started to sit down to make this list, some strange things happened—especially when I invited God to join me in making that list.

By this time, I had been venturing back to Sarasota from Hollywood every other weekend to help my old employer and friend with his ranch home. He was a guy that I thought I never wanted to see again, due to my resentment of how he took over the business that I had lost due to my addiction. In fact, it's funny that the *Big Book* has that exact resentment in it. It's on page 36 in the chapter called, "More About Alcoholism," in the first full paragraph. It says, "I came to work on a Tuesday morning. I remember I felt irritated that I had to be a salesman for a concern I once owned. I had a few words with the boss, but nothing serious."

Oh Jim, how I can relate to that on so many levels, plus, I love the downplay. Yeah, I had words with my employer, too—nothing serious. Just serious enough to cause a huge resentment in my life, plus the pain of wishing I could take back some of the words that I said out of anger.

My friend, Kurt, and I had a few words many times before. I hated him because he knew I was spiraling in my addiction and alcoholism and didn't do anything to help. To be very clear, before I got into recovery I felt that way about a lot of people I knew. A few years prior through the design industry, he and I had become best friends and he was one of our top clients before things blew up. We used to go shooting together on the weekends and did some fun things together.

We became close, but when things spiraled in my life and I couldn't carry on with the pressures of success, he took over the woodshop that I helped build, and our employees, so they could keep their jobs. He kept me on his staff, but I was watching what we had built go down in flames. There is more to the story, but the point is, when I went through a huge life event financially in my recovery, he made an offer to help me out. It required me coming back to Sarasota on weekends to help him do the woodwork on his ranch home.

Now I thought I would never see Sarasota again and I did not want to go. That was my lifelong habit of playing God, but it looked like God had other plans. It's true what my sponsor says, "I make plans, God laughs."

However, I don't believe I would have gotten as far with my amends without coming back to Sarasota. With the list of my amends in hand, I started making them. The first was this job with Kurt. When he took over the woodshop, he left me in charge. I had used our friendship as a means of getting away with doing a half-assed job by being the one in charge. However, my quality of work had gone down the drain, due to my drinking and drug use. I let him down and cost the company money, so when I finally left, it was not on very good terms.

Now that I was not only sober, but in recovery, I had on a new pair of glasses—the lenses weren't backwards anymore. He was trusting me to do the woodwork in his home to the best of my ability this time around. Because of my recovery, I was able to do that, and my new love for what I did was sparked by my fellow craftsman at ISM. I still can't thank Winfield and those guys enough.

I made the commitment to follow through every other weekend, so I would make the drive from Hollywood to Sarasota and help him out. I mean, he *did* help me out in a serious financial bind recently, so it was up to me to follow through on our deal. Every other weekend turned into every weekend. Then in April of

2023, my payback turned into a move back to Sarasota, so I could fully complete the job. Plus, my time was winding down at ISM, as the company was being restructured, so I wasn't very sure about my job security.

When I got back to Sarasota on one of those weekend trips, I ran into someone who wasn't on my list. It's funny how God works. Kurt and I went by my old woodshop—the one he had taken over and decided to sell. We were going to inventory things to decide what we wanted to keep or sell.

I had this neighbor at my woodshop a few bays down, who also did CNC work. Before I left Kurt's company, I had taken a side job with him. I had him cut some special inserts for this table I made, but I guess in my drug-fueled haze, I never paid the guy. I must have let it slip or just said it wasn't important. I was surprised to see him standing there.

He said to me, "What's up man?"

He held out his hand, like he was waiting for something, so I gave him a slap on the hand and said, "What's up!"

He said firmly "No, where's the money you owe me?"

Uh-oh … I asked him how much I owed him. When he told me, I happily paid him, but I felt horrible. This guy had always helped me out in a bind when I needed something specially made and I had left him hanging. I made it right, but I could feel God giving a chuckle in amusement. I can't blame God for that moment. After all, I had invited Him into this process.

My next amends came with my daughter, Miranda. Now in my run, I was not a great father. I used my dad as an excuse. I kept telling her during my run, "Well, at least I'm around, because my father never was."

I was there, but I wasn't present. How could a father be so cold and heartless to his sweet loving daughter? When the two of us would make plans for the weekend, I would tell her I was too tired and worn out. That was the truth, as I spent the whole week drinking and using drugs after work every day. I would try to spend the weekends detoxing, asleep on the couch 24/7, with a firm resolution that when I woke up on Monday, I would be able to stay sober for good. Mondays would come and go without any success.

That was the pattern for a couple of years. I know I let her down and hurt her. When she and her mother would try to wake me up, I would be angry that I had to get up. I wasn't verbally abusive, but I gave them a bad sense of insecurity. They never knew what mood I would be in, so I made them feel like they had to walk on eggshells in their own home.

I was guilt-stricken when I realized all of this. There was more neglect during that time, but now that I was moving back, it was time to start making up for it. The first way was an honest sit-down conversation with her. So one Sunday during a weekend visit, I had her mother drop her off at St. Armand's Circle in Sarasota, where there is some good shopping and dining. Miranda and I met for pizza and video games at an arcade we liked.

At pizza we talked. I told her that her mom said she was getting straight A's in school now and she nodded her head yes. Then I asked her why that was now.

She looked me in the eyes and said, "It's because you aren't home."

I swallowed hard. That was a very direct and honest answer. Look, my daughter is a very sweet, understanding, and caring young lady. We have always had this special bond, despite everything. Her answer didn't hurt me, but a sense of peace came over me. She and her mother could sleep better at night knowing that I was in recovery and in Alcoholics Anonymous. She finally had soulful peace of mind now that she didn't have to worry about my moods, which obviously caused her harm.

I smiled and said that I understood and was proud of her for her good grades. I also let her know that I respected her for being honest. Then I told her that I loved her and she said that she loved me, too.

I earned a new respect that day for my daughter and we have been rebuilding our bond ever since. It hasn't been easy, but part of my amends to her is to practice acceptance, to always be a better father, and to be happy that she has peace now. For Father's Day in 2023, she gave me the best gift ever. It wasn't something she bought. It was a tiny handwritten note that I have in front of me as I'm writing this. I cherish this note. It's priceless to me. It says.

> Dear Dad,
>
> Happy Father's Day!!! A year ago today you were on your journey to becoming sober, but now it's been one year and I couldn't be happier for you! You have come so far this past year and I believe that you will continue this journey for the rest of your life. You are a great dad and I love you so much. Happy Father's Day to you and I hope you have a fantastic day. Congratulations!"

Wow. That note left me speechless and I'm so grateful for her. I've always known she was a gift from God—later I have another story to share about an honest conversation we had. However, I'd like to move on to other amends. My father is next.

As you have read earlier, my father and I didn't exactly have the best relationship in our entire lives. After I was out of treatment for some time, I called him up and we had one of the best conversations we had ever had experienced.

We joked about me being sober now. He said to me "The best part about being sober is, I have never seen a sober guy get a DUI!" We had a great laugh and enjoyed catching up with each other. Before we got off the phone that day, he said something I'll never forget. He said that he was proud of me and that he loved me. That hit me very hard. For the first time in my life I didn't feel his "I love you" was selfish. I told him I loved him, too.

After I moved back to Sarasota we started to meet up for dinners. Not often, but a lot more times than we ever had done before. He has been in my life more and he has gotten to see his granddaughter for the first time in years.

We have even gone to meetings together. He has come to hear me share my experience, strength, and hope, and I have gotten the great honor of hearing his experience, strength, and hope, when he spoke at a meeting. I even was granted the incredible honor of handing him his forty-two year medallion this past April.

He made jokes about that tattered Big Book of mine. He looked at it and asked me with a chuckle "What edition is that?" We had a good laugh. We have made amends I believe in our own way. My father is a man of few words when apologizing and I accept him for exactly who he is. We don't have the same religious, political, or worldly views, but he is my dad and I wouldn't be here without him.

No, seriously—when he spoke, he basically said I was a product of his own better thinking with my mother. When he told the story, instead of getting angry, I couldn't help but laugh and the whole meeting laughed, too. We are the same, but complete opposites. I am him and he is me and I'm grateful that he is my father. I now accept him for all that he is and isn't. Is our relationship perfect? Not even close, but it's OK today. I don't have to drink and take drugs over it. I just love him for who he is.

My mother is my next amends. Sometime around Christmas of 2023, the resentment towards my mother was weighing on me. I didn't necessarily have resentment anymore, but I knew I had to practice something more—I had to practice some forgiveness. That was a hard one.

I went on Facebook, found her, and reached out with a friend request and left a message, where I simply said, "Hi."

She asked if I made a mistake by reaching out to her. I told her no, because I was trying to put aside my pride and ego. Then I told her that I loved her. I was also very sorry that I had told her twenty-three years ago that I never wanted to see her or speak to her again. I let her know about my recovery and that I wanted to set things right with her. We talked back and forth and exchanged numbers.

We have talked more since then. When I go with my daughter and girlfriend up to Illinois soon, I am going to go see her. How will it turn out? I have no idea, but I can tell you this—no matter what her situation is or what she has been through, and I don't care who she is as a woman today, I will show her grace and compassion. I hope this reunion happens and if it does, no matter what, I would love an opportunity for her to also meet her granddaughter, whom she has never seen. I would also love to give her a hug and tell her that I love her.

This is where total acceptance comes into play. This is where letting go and letting God comes into play. She is my mother and if I don't practice forgiveness, things will never be right in my life. That resentment toward my mother has affected every relationship in my life and every marriage. It's time to let it go and work on getting life right. I'm OK with whatever outcome follows this event. I'm just happy I have a mother. I wouldn't be here without her.

I firmly believe there is nothing that can't be made right, if I practice honesty, open-mindedness, and willingness. Before I move on to Step 10 I would like to share one more amendment I have had to make in this journey. It's one that I had the most guilt over. This is to show you again that there is nothing to be afraid of, as we all do despicable things on the way to pitiful and incomprehensible demoralization.

When my ex-wife and I ran the woodshop, I had this amazing part-time employee named Jerry. He was brought to my shop by my friend, Luke, who also worked part-time for us. They were both smart, land surveyors by day and loved to woodwork. I remember the first time I met Jerry. Luke told me about him and said Jerry was interested in coming to work part-time. I said I was willing to meet and talk with him.

One day Luke was coming to the shop after work as usual to help out, so before he got there, I went to the bathroom. When I came out, Luke and this mountain of a man were working on a door that I was building that day. The man was enormous in size and considerably older than either of us, but he had this aura about him, as well as a huge jolly smile. He spoke with a southern accent and was very polite, but he was also very smart and deliberate with every bit of work he did.

I looked at Luke that day and said, "Well, I guess Jerry is working for us."

I laugh to this day about that moment. I never got to interview him, because he just jumped in to help. I loved Jerry. We both enjoyed classic rock and he was a wealth of knowledge. He was also kind, and polite—a good ol' boy from Georgia, who loved to work. He would call me weekly and ask if I had anything for him to do and I always did, so he was at the shop often.

When we purchased new equipment for the shop he helped set it up. He could read a technical manual and make sense of it, which I couldn't. He was with us part-time for four years. After the work started to dry up, we had to let him go, but he was OK with that. He would drop by the shop every once in a while just to talk music and hang out. I loved his laugh and his energy and we used to talk for hours.

But one day in 2021, he came by the shop and I could tell that something had changed. He had lost over a hundred pounds, so he looked hollow. He had been informed he had stage 4 cancer, so he didn't have long to live, He would be going up to Georgia soon to be with his family, as there was nothing more the doctors could do. When I offered to assist him with meal prep since he didn't know how to cook for himself, he happily agreed to let me help.

However, I never was able to help with that meal prep, because my drinking and drugging were more important. I put that before helping him out, so I ghosted him on that. I felt horrible, but how did I deal with that horrible feeling? I drank and drugged more.

Then my wife at the time asked me how he was doing. I said he wasn't good and that he had asked me to get him some medical marijuana to help him out. She had control of our money, so I asked her for some cash to get it for him. However, I never got it for him, but I spent it on my addiction instead. I felt horrible for so long about that. How could I do that to such a kind man? He never did anything wrong to me.

I dealt with that feeling of guilt by drinking and drugging more. It added to my spiral. He kept trying to reach out and I wasn't available. I never saw Jerry again. I always said to myself, "I'll reach out to him tomorrow." Tomorrow came and went and I never got back with him. I was guilt-stricken about my behavior and lies. He went back to Georgia and was with his family when he passed away.

My behavior and the lies tore me up even in early recovery. This was something for which I had to figure out a way to make amends, so I now donate anonymously to various cancer charities. It doesn't make what I did OK, but it's a good start. Perhaps someday someone else will be helped by my regular gift. In a way, those donations would make amends to my father, too, for what I said to him years earlier.

As I said, it doesn't make what I did OK, but this is about a new way of life for me moving forward. I regret those things that I did on the way to my pitiful and incomprehensible demoralization, but I know I can set the future right by doing the right thing now.

Sharing this story is important to help a newcomer see that there is nothing that can't be made right to some degree. In making these amends and sharing about them, one of the Step 9 promises continues to hold true in my life—the promise of no matter how far down the scale we have gone, we will see how our experience can benefit others.

Chapter Eleven

Step 10

Continued to take personal inventory and when we were wrong promptly admitted it.

This step holds a special place in my heart. On page 84 of the *Big Book*, in the second full paragraph, it says "We have entered the world of the Spirit. Our next function is to grow in understanding and effectiveness. This is not an overnight matter. It should continue for our lifetime." Then on page 85, in the first full paragraph, it says something interesting: "It is easy to let up on the spiritual program of action and rest on our laurels. We are headed for trouble if we do, for alcohol is a subtle foe.

We are not cured of alcoholism. What we really have is a daily reprieve contingent on the maintenance of our spiritual condition. Every day is a day when we must carry the vision of God's will into all of our activities. "How can I best serve Thee—Thy will (not mine) be done." These are thoughts which must go with us constantly. We can exercise our will power along this line all we wish. It is the proper use of the will.

Those are powerful statements and I've gotten pretty good at taking my own inventory in this process. I find value and peace in looking at my daily actions lately. I notice that when I'm in God's will, people aren't getting hurt. I've noticed that when I take inventory, I also look at my assets, too, and grow those.

At the beginning of my recovery that was not the case. I didn't know how to take inventory properly. I was really good at taking *other* people's inventory. That "*Big Book* thumper" sponsor I told you about earlier gave me a crash course early on about this step and how to apply it. He also had me start working on Step 11 which I will talk about soon. I'd like to share my early Step 10 experience with you, and then another story of how I realized the tenth step promises came true in my life.

When I was working with my "*Big Book* thumper" sponsor, my original "Sponsor in name only" and I were still talking back and forth. I believe I said earlier that he was a Vietnam Marine Corps veteran. I liked the guy, but it wasn't a good fit. However, we still sent old military pics back and forth and talked regularly.

Now in between those military texts, he would send me some things that I didn't find funny—various racial and political texts. I could never bring myself to say to him, "Hey, could you not send me that stuff." Some of what he would say to me would also irritate me. One night, he went too far. He sent me a picture of the president dressed as Hitler, and was asking me in a laughing manner, why I didn't respond. Also, I heard from someone in the program who told me that he wouldn't speak at a meeting, because too many people of color were present I didn't know for sure or care if that was true, but it was really bothering me

However, his Hitler text sent me over the edge. My soon to be ex-wife was Jewish, my daughter is part Jewish, and their grandmother is one of the Jewish people who survived Auschwitz. I didn't find it at all funny, so I called him up and unloaded on him. I took his inventory up one side and down the other, and then I hung up the phone.

Next, I called my sponsor at the time and told him what happened. He simply asked me "Well, do you feel better?" I said yes and no. He figured at that moment I should know about Step 10 and how to practice it. He then told me something I'll never forget. He said, "You have to call him or see him in person and make amends for your behavior."

I basically replied, "Wait, what? Why should I have to make amends for *his* racist behavior? He should have known better. How dare he send me those ... oh, wait."

Then it hit me. I never told him *not* to send that stuff. I was afraid of what he would say to me if I told him to stop. Also, in my life, and still a tiny bit today, I have a bad habit of letting things go for too long, until they build up and I pop.

I have gotten better about not letting that happen at this current stage in my recovery. However, back then, I didn't know how to draw a boundary or say anything at all. I am admitting it now, but to this day, I have had to learn the hard way about being willing to do that. I hadn't ever really put up boundaries my whole life, so this was the start of deprogramming *my* behavior.

I swallowed my pride and asked him the right way to make amends. He told me to go to this man and let him know I had acted out of character, which I did. This is about a new way of life and I have to smash old behavior. Next, I needed to apologize and let him know my role in what happened. I was not to take his inventory under any circumstances. So I called him up and asked if we could talk the next time I saw him at a meeting.

That time was the very next day. When I saw him, I swallowed my huge ego and pride, spoke with him, and made amends. I was wrong and apologizing was better than the temporary satisfaction I received from yelling at him the previous night. As I said, I've had to learn the hard way that anger doesn't ever fix the issue or solve a problem—this was the start of that journey. We shook hands and to this day we are still cool.

I'm happy to have learned about Step 10 that day and had the opportunity to work it in my life. I was basically taught that we are never too early to put that step into action, as long as I know how to use it properly. Now later down the road, when I was with my official sponsor, as we went through it in the *Big Book*, I finally understood the essence of it. Alcohol is a subtle foe and resentment can invite that sneaky enemy into this new house of recovery that

I'm building. That foe is always waiting to come in, because I am never cured of alcoholism. But as long as I keep it up with self, God, and others, I'm that much further away from it.

In 2023, during the time that I was visiting in Sarasota and back to work on my friend Kurt's ranch, I was enlisted in creating a massive back bar in his butler's pantry. It was to be something that I designed with his input that would display his massive liquor collection.

Now Kurt isn't one of us alcoholics. He is a normal drinker and he loves to entertain. His liquor collection is huge and it was an honor to make that back bar for him. It took a couple of weeks to design it out and create it from concept to finish, but it came out beautifully. It's made from three huge reclaimed antique cabinets to hold his glasses. In between those cabinets I took this very old cove huge crown molding and set it vertically in strips, then encased the walls with them. I cut the strips into specific lengths to break them up, and inside of those cuts, I laid in thick glass shelves. It was some of my best work at the ranch—elegant yet rustic.

As I was putting on the finishing touches on this back bar, he started to set up the liquor displays. Now he is a designer by trade, but I have to say, for being a designer, he doesn't know how to display liquor worth a damn.

I watched him get started and after a while I said to him, "Really? That's how you are going to display these awful bottles for your guests? That's all wrong! Why are you going to display half-drank cheap liquor like that? Go get the good stuff and let me show you how it's done! Trust me I'm an alcoholic!"

He went and grabbed all the good stuff, while I helped set up the display. As we were setting it up, we were laughing and having a great time. Then it hit me. I realized what had just happened and the tenth step promises came true—or at least some of them.

Now if you are new to this program or aren't in it, the Step 10 promises start on page 84 of the *Big Book* and in the last paragraph it says: "And we have ceased fighting anything or anyone—even alcohol. For this time sanity will have returned. We will seldom be interested in liquor. If tempted, we recoil from it as from a hot flame. We react sanely and normally, and we will find that this has happened automatically. We will see that our new attitude toward liquor has been given to us without any thought or effort on our part. It just comes! That is the miracle of it. We are not fighting it, neither are we avoiding temptation. We feel as though we had been placed in a position of neutrality—safe and protected. We have not even sworn off. Instead the problem has been removed. It does not exist for us. We are neither cocky nor are we afraid. That is our experience. That is how we react as long as we keep in fit spiritual condition."

That is exactly how I handled seeing all that liquor that day. It never crossed my mind to take a drink. I wasn't cocky or afraid. I didn't even tell myself not to take a drink or that I'd better ask God to protect me from drinking while working on the setup of that bar. God had already been doing that.

I didn't fight it, and I didn't avoid temptation. That new attitude was just there. I had been doing the maintenance in my life to stay spiritually fit. I'm grateful for that day and that experience. Just because I got sober and entered recovery doesn't mean the world is going to make liquor go away. It's all around us, at every turn.

I used to think isolation was the solution to quitting drinking, and staying stopped. Turns out that the steps, a good sponsor, the fellowship, and a loving and caring Higher Power that I choose to call God is the solution.

Chapter Twelve

Step 11

Sought through prayer and meditation
to improve our conscious contact with
God as we understood Him, praying only
for the knowledge of his will for us
and the power to carry that out.

Whenever I think of this step and my introduction to it, I immediately think of one line in the *Big Book*. On page 88, last paragraph: "We alcoholics are undisciplined."

When I had that "*Big Book* thumper" sponsor, he knew what I didn't know, as I said earlier—that I had a conscious separation from God and needed to build a conscious contact with God or some form of a Higher Power immediately. When I met him, he asked me a very important question: "Do you get on your knees to pray?" I responded with a quick, "No!" He said in return, "That's OK! God loves you anyway."

That hit me hard. I never felt like God loved me. In fact, as I said earlier, I felt God was punishing me. I only prayed to God when I needed a favor and when God didn't deliver in a way I found satisfactory, I fired him temporarily. My best example was when I got arrested for my DUI in 2012. After I passed the field sobriety test with flying colors, one of the police officers had the guts to handcuff me and throw me into the back of their cruiser.

I couldn't believe it. I even let them know how well I was doing while the test was happening. How could they be so mean? Now here is how I know that I'm an alcoholic to my core. At no time during that traffic stop did I think, "Maybe I shouldn't have had those drinks earlier." My only thoughts were, "If only I hadn't taken I-75 at 2 a.m., they wouldn't have stopped me!" Also the thought of, "Why are they worried about what I'm doing? Don't they have real crimes to go take care of?" Never mind the fact that I passed out at the wheel, and swerved across three lanes of traffic. Thank God, it wasn't during the day and there was minimal traffic. Things could have been much worse, but I didn't see it that way at the time. When I landed in the back of the cruiser, I was so angry. With my hands cuffed behind my back and before the officer got into the car, I prayed to God out loud and said, "God, if you get me out of this, I won't ever drink and drive again!" Well, I went to jail.

On the way to the Manatee County jail, I let that officer know exactly what I thought of her. When we got to the jail, the intake officers were nice, but the female officer was the one who booked me, so I hated her. When they took me into the room to blow into the breathalyzer, I refused three times. I made sure to let them know I wasn't drunk, and there was no way I was going to put my mouth on their dirty, old, out-of-date, robot thingy. They said I would lose my license. I was livid by that point. I told them to take it, because there was no way in hell my mouth was going anywhere near their machine. Didn't they know who I was? Well, they called my bluff and took my license—I couldn't believe it.

I was thrown into a holding cell with three other guys. While walking up to the cell, two of the guys were awake, and the one on the top bunk on my side was passed out. Damn, that guy must be an alcoholic, as I could smell the liquor coming off him when I walked up to the cell—he smelled horrible. The other two gentlemen were already up and working out. It was about 4:30 a.m. by this point. I looked at them and they looked at me. I asked them what they were in for, and they both had the same story. Their girlfriends said they hit them. Of course, they didn't do it.

They asked what I was in for and I told them a DUI. They said "Well, you don't look drunk!"

I quickly replied, "I KNOW, RIGHT?"

Then I saw breakfast was coming, so I said, "Look, I've never been locked up before, but I've seen plenty of episodes of Lockup on MSNBC and so when that breakfast gets here, you guys can have it. I'm not hungry. Don't shank me."

They laughed and said, "OK!"

I made two friends right off the bat. We had a great time that morning. They gave me the rundown of the joint, we did a jailhouse workout, and I lost my socks in a game of checkers, but before I knew it, I was getting bailed out by my wife. She drove me to see an attorney immediately—she had just gotten the car out of impound.

That's right—we shared a car at the time. This was before the days of Uber, so she had to take my daughter to preschool in a taxi, and then take that taxi to the impound lot to get the car out. I'm sure that was a *great* morning for her.

I told my attorney the story of the DUI and he said to me, "Well, good thing you weren't drunk, because we will just pull the tapes from the traffic stop to prove you weren't."

I immediately thought, "Uh oh!" I started to get mad at God because he was supposed to get me out of this with zero consequences. That was our deal. I never ended up hiring that attorney and went to court anyway. I lost my license for a year, and had to pay a lot of money. I was also ordered to do community service and placed on probation. Our car insurance tripled.

Well, screw you, God! My promises that I made to God during those prayers, if he got me out of that situation, went by the wayside. My promise of never drinking again became, "Well, I'll just never drink and drive again." Then, by the end of my drinking career, that went away, too, but I'm lucky I never got a second DUI.

This was just one instance of where I only prayed for personal gain and for my own selfishness. This time around it was to be different in my recovery. When that *Big Book* thumper" sponsor got me to start praying, I thought he was crazy. How would prayer help me? He also had me start reading page 86 from the *Big Book* when I first woke up and when I retired. That's when I noticed something strange started to happen.

I began to feel a new peace flow in slowly. Not a lot of peace—just some. I started to inch a little closer to my Higher Power. It took a while still for me to believe totally in this Higher Power, but it paved the way for me to move closer to God.

Now in the beginning, I said that I didn't get on my knees, and he never made me do that. He knew I wasn't ready. Even when I started working with my official sponsor, he never made me kneel. However, what I did do was fellowship with God every morning, throughout my day, and at night before bed.

As I said before, I never really talked to God. I looked at Him as someone who would help me out of a jam and then punish me or not help me the way I thought He should. This time things were different. I started to build a friendship with my Higher Power.

After I was working with my current sponsor for a short while, I can remember being stuck in a nighttime traffic jam in Aventura, Florida, on the way to the 8:30 meeting at the Stirling Room. Traffic was bumper to bumper and at a dead stop, so I called my sponsor, frustrated that I was going to miss the meeting that night. He said something I'll never forget. "That's good! Thank you, God!" I had to ask him again what he said, so he said it again.

I asked him why he said that and he replied, "Because you need to start saying, *Thank you, God,* more often." He explained it to me right there on the spot, over the phone. It made sense—he was right. I should thank God *in* the good and in the bad and *for* the good and for the bad. That little exercise and short prayer means so much to me today.

After we hung up, I said, "Thank you, God." Then something strange happened. I reached a point in the traffic where I could turn into the parking lot of a local Target store. After I pulled out of traffic into the parking lot, I went inside the store. I wasn't going anywhere in particular anytime soon, so maybe I should just make the best of it. I went inside and walked around.

By this time in my recovery, I had an efficiency apartment in Hollywood. I loved that little place. While I was walking around, I found some good (yet cheap) storage cubes with some cool foldable cloth bins to fit. I located some curtains for my one window and a good sale on some basic kitchen items that I needed. I was happy as I walked out to my car and loaded everything up. I proceeded to pull back out onto the road and now, the traffic was clear. I went back to my apartment and spent the night assembling storage cubes and really started to set up my tiny apartment to officially make it my home. I went to bed that night feeling peaceful and a little closer to God.

That simple, short prayer became part of my daily routine in many situations and I noticed something strange happening. I was less irritable in that crazy Miami traffic. I was even less irritable when I had to wait in lines anywhere and I started to become less upset in situations that would normally send me off the deep end. God was growing in my life, in my heart, and in my soul. I still say that short prayer to this very day regularly. I still have fellowship with God every day and my prayer life has gotten stronger.

I have even started dropping to my knees more—not a lot, but more than I used to do. Sometimes I pray only for the knowledge of His will and the power to carry that out. I even find myself praying for others. I'm not perfect by any means today, but I do believe God has my best interest and that of others around me in mind. The set-aside prayer has become a big part of my recovery and it works wonders. I've even passed that on to my sponsees and also the simple Thank You, God prayer to other people. It works—it really does.

I used to feel faith and prayer were tools of inferiors. Now I see that it's the way to peace and strength. Page 100 of the *Big Book* says it best, where in the first full paragraph says, "Both you and the man must walk day by day in the path of spiritual progress. If you persist, remarkable things will happen. When we look back, we realize that the things which came to us when we put ourselves in God's hands were better than anything we could have planned. Follow the dictates of a Higher Power and you will presently live in a new and wonderful world, no matter what your present circumstances!"

Thank you, God!

Chapter Thirteen

Step 12

Having had a spiritual awakening as the result of these steps, we tried to carry this message to other alcoholics, and to practice these principles in all our affairs.

This step was the one that I was the most excited to experience when the time came. I have learned over almost a year later from that excitement what this step actually means to me. I will happily talk about that later on, before my book comes to a close. Until then, I think of page 89 in the *Big Book* when I think of my beginnings with this step, which says:

> Practical experience shows that nothing will so much insure immunity from drinking as intensive work with other alcoholics. It works when other activities fail. This is our *twelfth suggestion*. Carry this message to other alcoholics! You can help when no one else can. You can secure their confidence when others fail. Remember they are very ill.
>
> Life will take on new meaning. To watch people recover, to see them help others, to watch loneliness vanish, to see a fellowship grow up about you, to have a host of friends—this is an experience you must not miss. We know you will not want to miss it. Frequent contact with

newcomers and with each other is the bright spot of our lives.

I love that passage. Today I know it to be true, but that wasn't really my experience when I started working with others. The page that best explains my experience, when I started working with others, is page 96. The first paragraph says:

> Do not be discouraged if your prospect does not respond at once. Search out another alcoholic and try again. You are sure to find someone desperate enough to accept with eagerness what you offer. We find it a waste of time to keep chasing a man who cannot or will not work with you. If you leave such a person alone, he may soon become convinced that he cannot recover by himself. To spend too much time on any one situation is to deny some other alcoholic an opportunity to live and be happy. One of our Fellowship failed entirely with his first half dozen prospects. He often says that if he had continued to work on them, he might have deprived many others, who have since recovered, of their chance.

Yeah that sounds about right. I remember my first sponsee. I was so excited to be a sponsor and very eager to help others. It truly is a necessity to pass on what I've learned to others.

When my first potential sponsee approached me, I was more than willing to help. He was a young guy who was just coming back from a relapse. He had let everyone know about the three hundred and some odd sober days that he had strung together previously. He heard me share during a meeting that I was chairing and asked me after the meeting if I would consider sponsoring him.

First, I asked him a very important question: "What lengths are you willing to go to?"

Of course, he replied, "ANY!" That was good to know. He obviously wanted what I had, so I said yes.

Look, I want to be clear about something. First off, that is a horrible question to ask a newcomer. Second, I found out real quick where "any lengths" stopped. It stopped with this guy, as soon as I asked him to meet up to go through the *Big Book*. What happened is I became his sponsor in name only—I know, I know, God has good jokes!

I'd call him up and we make plans to meet up and start the step work. However, he wouldn't reach back out to me. He would show up to meetings late and not pay attention during them. He would call me to vent and ask life advice. I can even remember this one time when he called me to ask me for relationship advice. When he decided to come back into the program of recovery, he brought his girlfriend with him—that was from a previous time.

When I was on a trip back to Sarasota for one of my weekend work sessions at the ranch with Kurt, he called. He asked me if he should get back together with her, because they had just recently broken up. I immediately said, "Yeah, I'm an alcoholic and I've pretty much blown up every relationship that I've ever had."

He insisted that I answer, so I ended up replying, "OK, you want advice? Here's mine. Do what you want, because you are going to do it anyway."

I knew that to be true, because he reminded me of me, in my early recovery. I refused to have a sponsor that would tell me that I couldn't date. I had already dated several people in that first year. My first was not a rehab romance, but I met her at my treatment facility, which was a dual diagnosis place. I justified my relationship with this girl, because "she was just there for mental health only."

Yeah, you can imagine where that relationship went—nowhere quick. She took me on a ride of WTF that I still will never forget. I know I did the same in return to her. We had dated off and on in the first year of my recovery. I justified it every time, so I didn't learn my lesson. In fact, I justified it in another way, too. It was OK to date, as long as my meetings came first and my recovery was number one.

Now that I look back on that first year and wonder, what did I really have to offer anyone? I practiced the thirteenth step fully. That step is a great one. For those of you that don't know about that step, let me define it for you quickly. The Step 13 is basically Steps One and Twelve combined. My life is unmanageable and I want to share it with you. Dating in early recovery is like buying a used puzzle at a thrift store. Are all the pieces there? Guess we won't know until we try to put it together.

Anyway back to my first sponsee. So he ended up getting back into a relationship with her and completely blew me off. Then he got mad at me, because I didn't call him to help him with his Step work. His newcomer girlfriend went back out, and all kinds of chaos ensued.

OK, first off, it works if YOU work it. It doesn't work if your sponsor works it for you. When I worked with my sponsor, as I recall, I was the one who had to call and ask to get together. I had to be the motivated one and it was passed on to me that we don't chase sponsees. I can't keep someone sober. If they don't want to put in the work to get better, then that is on them. I know I spent many hours with my sponsor, in the book, in one-on-one discussions, and in meetings (on time). My recovery became very solid, because of a solid routine and a whole lot of honesty, open-mindedness, and willingness.

The last straw with that first sponsee was when he called me to take my inventory, because I wasn't paying enough attention to him. I even gave him "bad relationship advice." He also informed me that out of all the sponsors he's had, I was the worst according to him.

I ended up telling him that maybe it was best he found a new sponsor. He did, and from what I hear, he is sober to this day. I am happy that he found the person with whom he was meant to work. Has he dived fully into the *Big Book?* I don't know, but I hope he has or did, because that is where all the answers are.

After that first experience, I ended up working with various other men in the program. I partnered with a guy, who any time we read the *Big Book* and discuss something, he would tell me that he "already knew that." So he was basically unteachable and I had to break ties with him. It's really hard to help someone who is like that. Plus, I basically felt like I became his therapist, because he would only call me to complain about things happening in his personal life.

I remember back when I did that with my "*Big Book* thumper" sponsor, he would stop me on the phone and tell me, "Go to God." After I heard him say that a few times, I began to wonder why said it so much.

A couple of weeks later, we were in a meeting together and he was sharing. He said, "Yeah, basically whenever someone or a sponsee calls me and is spitting some BS out of their mouth, I tell them, "Go to God!"

Wait a second Big Book thumper sponsor, I thought. *You told* ***me*** *to "Go to God."* Ugh—ego deflated.

The last time I saw that former sponsee, he was still sober—maybe. The funny thing is when you have decent recovery, you can usually spot a dry drunk or someone who is white knuckling this program from pretty far away. I hope that he has found the person he can work with and will stick with a program of recovery.

I have worked with a couple of guys who ditched recovery around Step Four. I've had others who asked me to sponsor them, but after I said yes, that's as far as it went. For a while I became discouraged and wondered if this was how it was always going to be. Sponsoring guys is frustrating.

Then it happened—I finally received a solid sponsee—an angry one, but solid nevertheless. I could relate to this guy on so many levels. I knew very well of anger and sometimes still do—not as much, but sometimes. He reminded me of me in so many ways.

I was happy to work with him. In fact, we still have a sponsor/sponsee relationship to this very day. We have worked through each step deliberately, and I've watched him grow slowly. It really has been the bright spot of my life. I swear, too, that I didn't have gray hair before working with others. I think this guy gave it to me. Maybe it's a coincidence? I'm willing to bet not, but we will go with a "Yes" on that one.

We talk often and read together. Watching someone who really wants to learn and grow is priceless to me. In the last six months, I even picked up another sponsee. He is far along in the steps and is growing daily. He really loves to learn and grow, so I have been able to pass on things to him that Doc and others have given to me. It's a joy to see someone go from lost to found. He was even agnostic when we started working together. I didn't force him to believe—it just happened somehow.

I took my current sponsor's approach. I started him on the set-aside prayer and reading page 86 out of the *Big Book*. We created the list of attributes and I made sure to tell him that he could call his Higher Power anything and believe in whatever made sense to him. Now some may disagree with that approach but I have several reasons for that approach.

I know that if someone tried to force me to say the word, God, or believe like they believed, it would have turned me off to recovery. A friend of mine in the program once told me a story. He said that he had a friend whose higher power was a butterfly. After a few months of not talking to his friend, he called him up one day. He asked him, in a way that was making fun of him, "How's that butterfly of yours doing?"

He said that his friend replied, "Actually that butterfly grew into God." My friend said that he felt so small at that point. That story stuck with me.

I firmly believe that I can't judge a sponsee or anyone for their higher power. I've heard in the rooms that your Higher Power can't be a doorknob, because it will turn on you. I personally disagree. Maybe that doorknob symbolizes the door that particular person walked through in AA. I know for me, opening that door to the meeting room, when I finally got serious about recovery, was a huge deal. I would look forward to opening that door every day to get the recovery I craved and to fellowship with my new family and friends.

Besides, if I criticize that new person in recovery for having a doorknob for a Higher Power, I might prevent that doorknob from turning into God. I know in the beginning my Higher Power was a book called *The Art of Happiness* that I found on the bookshelf in treatment. It got me through the early tough times of recovery and was a great substitute until I truly found my Higher Power.

Eventually that Higher Power grew into God. I believe God put that book on that bookshelf so I could have a comfortable start in this journey and have a small start at real change. That book changed my life. I still pair it with my *Big Book* to this very day. I love to pair my spirituality with spirituality. So back to this new sponsee of mine.

I remember one day we were talking about his Higher Power and out of nowhere he said the word, "Him." I stopped and he stopped. It was almost like you could hear the record scratch happen. I simply said, "We are going to stop here for the day."

We both laughed and ever since then, I've watched him and his Higher Power grow hand in hand. It's been a huge bright spot in my life. Will this sponsee stay sober? I don't know what his future holds or what God has in store, but whatever that future is, I hope he at least knows that God always has his best interest in mind. I know that God has mine in mind.

Chapter Fourteen

Seasons and Reasons

Seasons and reasons are what I think of when I think of my dear friend, Volunteer Alex. Sometimes people come into our lives for a season or a reason—Volunteer Alex was both.

I can clearly remember the day that I met him. I had been a member of the West Dixie Club for only a short time. One Sunday morning, at the beginners meeting, this crazy looking guy was there. He had mid-length hair, a smile that was unmatched, and was more enthusiastic than anyone in the room. He was loud, outspoken, and happy. I kept looking at him in the meeting and thinking, "What is this guy on?"

After the meeting, I was standing outside fellowshipping with other alcoholics and he came up to me. My friend was his friend, too. We ended up talking for a brief minute before he asked me, "Which way are you going home?" I told him and he said, "Oh good, you can drop me off on the way!"

Before I could say no, he was already walking towards my car. *OK, God, looks like I'm dropping him off at home.* Turns out he stayed at the halfway house where several of my friends in early recovery were staying. We struck up a short conversation on the way, but it was a few days before I saw him again.

This time, the same thing happened. I ended up dropping him off again and we started talking about time and meetings. He had about six more months of sober time than me, and he loved meetings as much as I did. He had this look on his face when he talked about meetings that I had never seen on anyone's face before. He absolutely *loved* them—they excited him. He told me that he had been addicted to heroin and alcohol. He said this was his first time in recovery, so he started to tell me some of his story. We bonded instantly.

Alex had been through so much in his journey to surrender. He was grateful for every day that he now had. I began picking him up for meetings and giving him rides back to the halfway house regularly. Here's where I made the mistake of a lifetime. I exchanged phone numbers with him.

We talked often, and soon he started asking me to pick up him and some other guys for meetings. Sometimes I would go to a meeting by myself, but it never failed that my phone would ring before the meeting started—it was always Alex and, of course, he would ask me what meeting I was attending. If it was close to the halfway house, he would ask if I would come pick him up or he would say that a couple of guys in the house needed a meeting. I never said no. It was the first time I felt I was of real service within my first ninety days. Right before I hit ninety days, he asked me to come with him to a detox center and share my story.

I didn't have much to share, so I used the book, *The Art of Happiness*. I loved that book, since I wasn't proficient yet in the *Big Book*, so I was not able to offer a real message of hope and recovery yet. However, I did share what a specific passage in that book meant to me, and how it related to my journey so far. After I shared my story at detox that day, he got a huge smile on his face. We went to dinner afterwards, where he told me how he loved the way I was able to speak and relate to people. I dropped him off that night.

I saw him the following Sunday morning at the beginners meeting. He was the chairperson for the month. I was standing outside the door talking with other newcomers, when he swung the door open and came out. He came right up to me and pulled me aside. He asked if I had that book with me and I said, "Of course, I do!"

He said "Good, because my speaker didn't show and you are on in ten minutes!"

Wait, what? Yeah, that's how I got into speaking in recovery. Alex "volun-told" me. I was super nervous, but excited at the same time. He called me up as his speaker and I shared my story. Of course, it was mostly a problem, but I made it through.

After the meeting I got asked by a couple of different alcoholics to come share at another beginner's meeting, and another detox center. That is how things in recovery started to take off for me. I don't say that from an ego standpoint, but because when I started to be of service to my fellow alcoholics, it felt so good. As I began gaining some confidence, my recovery started to change. I craved more knowledge about this disease and the *Big Book*.

As time went on, Alex and I became close. I would pick him up daily for meetings after my job at the yacht company and we would ride together. We bonded over our love for music and he always cracked me up. He was such a funny guy. We were usually laughing over something.

I remember one day we were on our way to a 5:30 p.m., meeting when we got stuck in a huge traffic jam. I was looking on my phone for a better way to go, but Alex insisted that I put the phone away and trust that he knew the way. I objected, but he still insisted, so I finally put the phone down and said to him, "Fine, we will take your way."

Well, we arrived at the meeting 45 minutes later than we would have the other way! When we pulled up to the meeting, I looked at him and he looked at me. I had that look of frustration in my eye, but he looked at me and smiled.

Then he slapped me on the back of my shoulder and said, "My man! Look, we got here just in time to do the chips!" Then he opened the car door, got out, and walked into the meeting happy as can be. I sat in my car and let out a frustrated laugh and then went in, also. Just as I sat down, it was the end of the meeting, and it was time for the chips.

Any Lengths

Alex LOVED the chips. At the West Dixie and other club houses on the east coast of Florida, they do them a little differently. The chairperson always asks for a volunteer to do the chips. Then, after the volunteer does the chips, some tips are also offered for the newcomer. It's usually stuff like, "Do 90 in 90, get a sponsor, call your sponsor, or keep coming back." Well, anytime they would ask for a volunteer for the chips, before they could finish that sentence, Alex would always shout out, "I'LL DO THEM!"

This time it was different. Before the chairperson could finish the sentence, Alex yelled out, "MARK WILL DO THEM!"

Thanks Alex. Looks like I got volun-told into doing something new again. It seems like we arrived in just enough time for "Mark" to do the chips. When I went up to do them, I was nervous as if I had never done them before. However, I made it through and felt good afterwards. I also got to see why Alex loved doing the chips so much.

When he would do them, he would hold the one in his hand up high so everyone in the room could see the chip. He would have this proud look on his face. Then, he would smile big when someone came up to get one. He would ask them their name and give them a hug. He would then say their name out loud, announce their time, and start a round of applause. If nobody grabbed one for the month he was holding up, he would loudly yell, "WHAT DO WE DO?" Then everyone would answer, "Keep coming back!" That day, I gave out a chip, and I finally understood the feeling of giving someone a token of their early milestone. It's also important to understand why we do the chips and medallions.

Page 403 in the *Big Book* says it best. In the first paragraph, second sentence on page 403, in the story, "A Drunk Like You," the author says,

> Once I saw somebody get a ninety-day pin. I decided not to get one. Even though I couldn't see it from where I was sitting, I wasn't going to wear an AA sign. One day, somebody got a ninety-day pocket piece that he could rub for luck, and I decided to get one of those. After my

three months were up, I went to the literature guy and bought one. He said it would be nice if it was presented to me in front of everybody, but I wasn't too keen on getting up in front of everyone. He said it would be good for the newcomers, as it would show them that the program worked.

Getting those milestones are huge, not only for the person receiving them, but also for the newcomer. In the beginning, those chips are important, because years might not feel attainable to a newcomer, but a few months—sure, that's attainable.

I can remember when I was thirty days sober and saw someone pick up a sixty-day chip. I wondered what it would feel like to be at that sixty-day mark. It turns out, it felt better than the thirty days chip. Then the days turned into weeks and more weeks turned into months. At each little milestone, I felt better. The hardest wait was between the six-month and the nine-month chip. I was so happy to get the nine-month chip, because a year medallion was just around the corner.

I remember my six-month chip the most though, because it was Volunteer Alex who gave it to me at the West Dixie Club. He was so excited, he gave me a great big hug. The two of us and some good friends in the fellowship went out to dinner afterwards to celebrate. A good time was had by all.

After my six months passed, I started to dive into a lot of service work, such as chairing and speaking, but I also loved working behind the coffee bar at the Stirling Room. I also began working heavily with my current sponsor and Doc in the *Big Book*. Alex asked me a few times to come speak at different meetings. Well, let's back that statement up a bit. More like I was volun-told—as usual. In fact, that's how he got the name Volunteer Alex.

I looked at him one day while I was up sharing my journey through recovery and said, "That guy right there, Mr. Volunteer Alex, is the reason I'm up here today. So if you don't like what I have to share, see him after the meeting!"

He laughed so hard, as did others. The name stuck and others started calling him by that name. He volunteered me to work the coffee bar a few times, also. I loved watching Alex during a meeting. When myself or someone else would be speaking, he stayed focused on the share happening. He would get this wide-eyed look on his face, if the share started getting intense or was very good. His eyes would get even bigger, if it was something so good, but he had never heard before in recovery. He had this laugh when he heard something funny during a share that was just infectious to the room. Alex always said that he loved the newcomer—especially the person with the gift of desperation. He loved helping others and even became head of his halfway house.

As time passed, Alex and I didn't spend as much time together, but we stayed close. I was diving into the *Big Book* with my sponsor and Doc so much more. In fact, one day Alex and I were riding together and he said his sponsor was taking him through the steps quickly. I said, "Yeah? Here, then tell me about the 'Doctor's Opinion'!" and I then tossed my *Big Book* to him in the car.

He laughed and tossed it back. We tossed that book back and forth while riding down the road several times. In fact, that is how the front cover came off of my *Big Book,* which was already almost worn out.

I did ask him once if he was retaining the information in the *Big Book*. He told me that his sponsor was taking him through the *Big Book* and the Steps quickly, so he could start helping guys recover. I asked him again if he was retaining the info, but he really didn't say much. He laughed it off and so I dropped it and didn't bring it back up. It was his recovery, not mine.

Besides, Alex was doing way more service and more meetings than I was at the time. If I was doing two to three meetings a night, he was doing four. If I had a chair commitment, he had triple the service commitments that I did. Not that it was a recovery competition—it was just who Alex was. He loved helping others.

Right before I moved back to Sarasota in April of 2023, I saw Alex at a meeting. He was grabbing a coffee and wasn't looking too good. He didn't have that usual smile on his face, so I asked him if he was OK. His answer was, "Not really."

When I asked him if he needed to talk, we stepped outside. The meeting had already started, but we spent that next twenty minutes or so of it outside talking. He had quit smoking a few months before that, but he said that he had started smoking cigarettes again and he also said he was starting to isolate at his new halfway house. He had moved houses due to a dispute with another resident at his other house.

He also proceeded to tell me that he had a sponsee, who was in either Step Six or Step Eight. He felt like he didn't know how to help him properly. I asked him if he retained any of the knowledge that his sponsor had passed on to him, but he said, "No."

He told me that his sponsor had taken him through the steps rapidly at his own request, so he could jump out and help others ASAP. I looked at Alex in that moment and said, "You're gone before you know it." Then I asked him "What does help look like to you?"

He said he was afraid to tell others that he was struggling, because he was known as the guy who was doing so well in recovery. I said that didn't matter, because he needed to speak up and seek help.

He told me he knew that and would do so. I suggested maybe getting a new sponsor or taking time away from helping others, so he could help himself. He agreed, so we put our heads together and came up with a mutual name of someone we both trusted and who had a ton of knowledge and worked a very solid program of recovery.

He said that he would ask this gentleman to sponsor him. That was the last time I saw Alex before my move to Sarasota, but I still called to check on him a couple of times.

Then the week came in May when it was time for my one-year anniversary and I was so excited. It had been a month and half since I had seen any of my East Coast recovery family. I left

Sarasota and spent four days in North Miami, where I picked up my year at the West Dixie Club and the Stirling Room. I picked up my year several times in those four days at different meetings at the two club houses. It was important to show the newcomer it worked, if you worked it.

Alex invited me to the 7 a.m. Friday morning meeting at the West Dixie that weekend. They asked me if I wanted to pick up a medallion at that meeting and I agreed. When they asked me who would be presenting me, I looked right at Alex and said that he would be do it.

The look on Alex's face was priceless. He was so happy. I had never seen him hold up a medallion that high in the air before. He gave me a huge hug and was smiling from ear to ear. After the 9:30 a.m. meeting that morning, we took a picture together and went for breakfast at IHOP to see a mutual friend of ours who was serving tables there.

We had a huge breakfast and then walked to the truck I was driving. While we were on the way back to his halfway house, he was telling me how incredible his new sponsor was. He felt that he was learning a ton about recovery, and actually absorbing the *Big Book*.

We pulled up to his halfway house and said our goodbyes for the day. Then I asked him if he was coming to the meeting on Saturday morning. "Yes," he said with a big smile. He walked into the house and that was the last I saw of him that weekend.

I was happy for my friend, but he didn't show for that Saturday meeting. I just figured he had something come up that Saturday morning, so he wasn't able to make it. I finished out the weekend and drove back to Sarasota that Sunday night. It was an incredible weekend and was so good to see the many people who had a huge influence on my recovery in my first year. I missed my East Coast recovery family already. However, I was excited, because after I picked up my year that Saturday morning, I was asked to speak at a meeting in June at a clubhouse that I had never spoken to before.

One morning about two weeks before that mid-June date, I got a call. from my friend, Sarah. She told me that Alex was dead. It took me a minute—I didn't believe her at first. We were both very close to Alex. I asked her if someone had hit him on the new scooter he had just bought.

She said, "No, he overdosed." I was in total shock and couldn't believe it. She told me the story she was told and it broke my heart. He had been found dead in his room at the halfway house by a mutual friend of ours.

I called up the mutual friend who had found him and he confirmed the story. He also gave me other details. I was heartbroken and so were many others. I felt lost inside. I immediately looked at the picture of us that was taken of him giving me my one-year medallion. That was the only picture Alex and I ever had taken together. I was so glad that something told me that morning to have that picture taken. I'm so happy that I did.

I asked to stay informed of when the celebration of his life was scheduled, so I got the news that it was the day after I was scheduled to speak at this meeting in June. Therefore, I made plans to stay in North Miami for the whole rest of the week and for the weekend.

I went and spoke at the June meeting. Then, I went to Alex's celebration of life. It was a great reunion of friends in recovery. I was able to see two things that day—the first being the love of AA and the second was how going back out and not getting the chance to come back affects others.

I learned that grief and gratitude go hand in hand. I was grateful for the reason and the season that I got to spend with Alex, but yet filled with sorrow that I would never get to spend another minute with him to experience his energy, his joy, and that smile and his laugh. I already missed not being volun-told to do things in recovery. His celebration of life was packed with recovering alcoholics and addicts, all of whom he touched in some special way. That's the thing about being gone. You don't get to see who you truly impacted in life and or how those people really feel about you.

I had the chance to stand up and share a few quick stories about Alex. There was laughter and joy. Others got up to share their favorite Alex stories and there was more laughter and joy. He brought a lot of people together that day. The funeral was the next day, but I couldn't bring myself to go to it. That was *not* the last memory I wanted to have of Alex. However, I did go to a meeting though and *did* the chips.

The rest of the weekend passed and I went back to Sarasota. I was grateful to get to experience Volunteer Alex for that time in my life. My recovery wouldn't have been the same without him.

I remember a good friend in the program once told me that we could make amends to those who have passed in life, since maybe we didn't get to say all we wanted to say. I never was able to truly tell Alex how much he meant to me, how much I loved him, and how grateful I was for him, so when I got back to Sarasota I thought about it. I first thought I would write to him, but I wondered how he would get that letter, so I sent a text to his phone instead. I still have it saved on my phone today and this is what the text said:

Alex I wanted to thank you for your friendship and for helping me in the program. I don't know what happened before you passed or what was going through your head or the struggle you must have been facing, but I want you to know you are truly missed already. Thank you for volunteering me to start doing the chips, for volunteering me to start speaking, and for that time you volunteered me to work the coffee bar. You helped me into doing service and your reasoning motivated me always. You were the best human GPS every time we went out somewhere, lol. You helped so many and gave so many others hope. Maybe it was your time and God needed someone to chair a meeting in heaven or to work the coffee bar or to do the chips. I'm happy you get to be an angel now and that your struggles are over. I know you're already making fast friends up there and have probably already been to a few meetings. Heaven is lucky to have a great guy with so much motivation. Thank you from the bottom of my heart for the great times, the laughs, and the friendship that I'll carry with me for the rest of my days here on earth. I'll see you someday at that meeting in heaven and I'm ready for whatever service you're going to volunteer me for. I'm hoping this message reaches you and you are finally at peace. See you someday, my friend. I love you more than I could have ever told you and many others love you, too. Travel easy.

The reason I wanted to share that text is simple. My sponsor during that time helped me with being able to mourn his passing properly. I had never done that in my life up until this point. When friends would pass, I would always use their death as a great excuse to drink and use drugs. I remember when my grandfather, who raised me, passed away in 2020. Well, not really, because I spent a month drunk and high on cocaine to help avoid the feelings of grief.

My sponsor told me that it is selfish to want someone all to ourselves here on Earth. God wants to enjoy his creation, too. He also shared with me that instead of getting to pray for Alex, I got to pray to him, and that was beautiful, because he was now an angel. His pain and struggles were over.

It was a shame how he passed and I can't imagine the pain a heroin addict goes through trying to get sober and stay sober. I have heard it's one of the hardest things ever. That was never my drug of choice, because even though I am heavily tattooed, I am terrified of needles.

It was hard to quit cocaine and alcohol but I have heard that heroin is way worse to recover from. It's a shame that so many never get a chance to experience recovery or fully recover. It's always hard, when someone you are close to in recovery goes back out and doesn't make it back.

My sponsor is right though—it is beautiful that I can talk to my friend any time I want now. I speak with him daily. Whenever I go over to the West Dixie Club or Miami, I think of him and can feel his presence every time I walk into that clubhouse. I miss seeing him behind the coffee bar. I miss that smile and laugh in meetings, but I feel him there with me.

I even acquired a tattoo in his memory. My tattoo artist is in early recovery. He said that tattoos are about healing and the journey in life. After Alex passed, I got a tattoo on my right shoulder blade. It's of a six-month blue poker chip that has wings. In the middle of the circular poker chip is a triangle that has the initials V.A. for Volunteer Alex. It symbolizes recovery—the chips, which were his favorite, are the six-month chip he gave to me and the wings symbolize that he is an angel now.

I had it placed on my right shoulder blade because I know he always has my back, just like I always had his, while he was here. I miss my friend and I can't wait to see him at that huge meeting in the sky. I know he is saving a seat for me.

Chapter Fifteen

The Spiritual Awakening

The funny thing about Step 12 is that it doesn't say having had a quick spiritual awakening, a non-chaotic spiritual awakening, an easy spiritual awakening, or even a peaceful spiritual awakening. It simply says, "Having had a spiritual awakening as a result of these steps."

I believe my spiritual awakening began in October of 2023, about six months after "completing" the steps. I put that in parenthesis, because are we truly ever done with them?

At this point, I had been with my new girlfriend for about two months and we were off to a great start. She was a woman that I had known from years prior and we reconnected. She was never a part of my active addiction or alcoholism, so I don't think she was aware of the path that I had traveled until I told her.

She is not like me. She is the type of woman who can have a couple of drinks and stop. I know, right? That still blows my mind to this day. My hat is off to any "normal" drinkers.

This one time I went out to dinner with friends, which was right before my girlfriend and I reconnected. The guy next to me was asked a very common question by our server, as she asked him if he wanted another round.

He gave her a very strange answer. He replied, "No thanks, I've had two already, so I'll have water instead."

When I looked at him, he looked at me, and I laughed. I said to him "You know it still blows my mind to this day how some people are able to do that!" We had a great laugh.

OK, now back to the spiritual awakening.

My girlfriend and I went for coffee one rainy afternoon in south Sarasota. After we spent some time in the coffee shop sipping our cups and talking, we decided it was time to leave. We walked outside to the parking lot and hugged in the light sprinkle of rain that was drizzling down.

As we were hugging, I saw a man pushing a huge road case down the highway, with clothes piled on top and a guitar on top of that. Now for those of you who don't know what a road case is, I'll tell you. It's a large black case with wheels on it that bands use to pack gear in while on tour. The one this young man was pushing was quite large.

He was probably in his twenties with long stringy hair. He was skinny and you could tell he was a traveler. As he was pushing this case down the road in the rain, he shouted out to me, in the middle of this embrace with my girlfriend, "HEY! Would you be able to help me with a few dollars, so I can get an iced tea or something to drink?"

I replied back, "I'm sorry, but I don't have any cash on me."

He then asked, "Well, there's a corner store right over there across the street, so could you still help me out?"

I looked at my girlfriend and told her to wait in the car, while I was helping this guy.

Then, I told the stranger, "Meet me over there!" He happily pushed his case over to the corner store and waited for a minute. Now before I continue on, I would like to lay out why I helped him.

For one thing, I don't mind helping a traveling musician, but another reason why is because my sponsor taught me some important life tips—if I'm in a position to help others, I should. We never know when God shows up. He can take many forms and likes to drop in on us to see how we are living. I believe this to be true. It's happened several times to me, now that I look back at certain spiritual experiences. This one was different though.

I made the ten-second drive over to that corner store, told my girlfriend that I would be just a minute, got out of my car, and went over to the corner store. The stranger was already standing there, so I said, "Come inside with me."

Then I went into that store with the intention for him to pick out what he wanted and I would just purchase it for him. Instead, I changed my mind and went to the ATM, pulled out a twenty dollar bill, and handed it to him. I told him to get himself some food, too.

With a smile on his face, he requested something very strange. He asked me, "Can I pray with you?"

Immediately my ego started to swell. Before I could think of the best prayer to recite for us, this stranger put one hand on my right shoulder and his left hand on my other shoulder right behind my neck, and demanded with authority, "ON YOUR KNEES!"

Then he pushed me down to my knees and he got down on his knees, also. This young man proceeded to rip a prayer with such intensity and enthusiasm that it was absolutely incredible. He didn't care who was in that store or who was listening or watching. I had never heard anyone pray with this kind of passion before.

It wasn't only the prayer that got me, but what this young man said in the middle of it. He prayed: "Protect this man from the disease that centers in his mind." Then he just kept on going. When he was done, he pulled me up and said, "Now, take that seed I've just given you and go water it with love. Don't ever water it with vinegar!"

I was in shock at what just happened. I felt strangely at peace and calm inside—calmer than I had ever felt in my entire life. I walked out of that store without saying a word. I got into my car and sat there stunned.

Then there was a knock at my window. It was the young man who had just finished praying with me. I rolled down the passenger side window and he said, "Don't forget what I just told you! Water that seed with love—not vinegar!"

I asked him if he needed a ride somewhere, but he replied, "No, I've already got a ride."

I asked him where he was headed to and he replied, "I don't know—maybe Israel!"

I said, "OK," rolled up my window, and backed out. He was gone in a flash.

I drove home that day feeling more at peace with myself and the world than I had ever felt before. I told my girlfriend what happened inside the store and her mind was blown.

She said, "It sounds like he was looking for someone to be kind to him."

I agreed, but I don't know about anyone else—I felt that was God showing up. For what purpose I had no idea.

What I can tell you is that about a week before that, I was talking with God during some prayer time. I admitted to Him that I wasn't getting on my knees to pray as much and asked if he could help me—so there's that.

Another month passed and I was asked to speak on Veterans Day at a spiritual meeting, which was on Steps 3, 7, and 11. I told the fellowship my story of the young man who asked me to pray with him. I just couldn't get it out of my head—that feeling of peace and serenity.

Weeks later, it still stuck with me. Thanksgiving and Christmas came and went. After New Year's, my girlfriend and I started having problems. I had a hard time seeing eye-to-eye with her.

I was also going to Miami for meetings every chance that I could. Those trips would take the whole weekend. I still loved those meetings on the east coast of Florida, so I would spend any free time there. I would make the three-hour drive there and another three hours back every other weekend or more. I was also attending at least a meeting here in Sarasota daily or, if the day was right, two meetings a night.

I was spending any other free time with my daughter, Miranda, or working overtime, so I was completely drifting in my relationship with my girlfriend. I ended up calling it off with her officially in February, right before my birthday.

I was fine at first, but ended up missing her after a couple of weeks. I went back to see if we could work things out. Now in that last statement lies my defect of character. I wanted to work things out, but was making myself unavailable. She agreed that we would give it another try, but I wouldn't move back into her home right away. Right before we broke up, I had lived with her and her two daughters for about a month.

For the next month and a half we dated and then decided to try to live together again. I was excited, but then work had taken over my life, so I was still going to Miami every chance that I had for meetings and fellowship. I told her that I would follow through better this time when I made commitments at home and with us. However, I was starting to get restless again.

When I started trying to be at home with her again, I would look for any opportunity to stay away. I didn't follow through with anything that I had promised her. Every time anyone from the fellowship would call and ask me to do a last-minute service, I would go—I never said no. If we had plans for a date, I would end the evening early, so I could perform the service or cancel plans altogether.

By June I felt really off, as I was wrestling with turmoil at my job, my relationship with my daughter, and my home life. I kept asking God for help, for the knowledge of His will, and for the power to carry that out. Even though I was staying very active in the fellowship, I felt that my life had become unmanageable in a different way. I couldn't get a grasp on balance—things had become chaotic.

I kept praying but didn't feel I was finding any answers, so I did what any reasonable alcoholic would do. I wrote God an email. I'm serious. I sat down and typed out a letter, because I wasn't even sure how God would receive a mailed letter. I don't have God's email address, but before I typed out this letter, I prayed and said out loud, "Well, God, I hope you get email!"

I typed out the letter and stuck it into a folder on my computer. In that letter, which is so personal to me, I laid out how restless I was feeling and how I felt like my recovery wasn't whole—for some reason, it had plateaued. I wasn't feeling able to help others effectively. I laid out how my work and home life balance was off. I asked God to intervene and help.

I was in pain and starting to step backwards mentally. Now I know this may seem crazy to some of you, but this was what I did in a moment of desperation.

I had spent so many years of my life before recovery being an active workaholic. I was never home for many years during my marriage—the thought of "How did I get back here again?" was eating me alive.

My current sponsor and I talk about this regularly. It says in the "Doctor's Opinion" on page xxviii, in the first full paragraph, "These allergic types can never safely use alcohol in any form at all."

Alcohol for me in recovery can be anything from self-pity to anger to sadness, and then back to alcohol and drugs. I've really had to watch my thoughts carefully. If I'm feeling off, sometimes I try to numb things in certain ways. Since alcohol or drugs isn't an option, I can easily become a spendaholic, a workaholic, or just shut down completely. As I was going into this phase of my recovery, I started eating my feelings. I had gained about thirty-five extra pounds.

I am the type of person who can become stuck in self-pity, if I don't catch it fast enough. Otherwise, I'll stamp down on myself for actions and thoughts. I'll begin beating myself up and won't stop until it's too late. I do my best to take inventory throughout the day, but if my thoughts went the wrong way, I become really hard on myself. So for me, it starts by getting drunk on self-pity. Then I start trying to correct things without pausing and praying, so I second-guess myself.

A lot of that comes from never dealing with life properly for most of my adult existence. My solution was always a drink or drug and that's not an option anymore for this alcoholic. The reality is, I am way better than I used to be, but if I get unbalanced, that's when things get unmanageable.

To be even more honest, I hadn't really had a serious relationship in recovery until now either. I tried and always failed spectacularly. I know, right? This goes back to that whole thing about why I don't give relationship advice to my sponsees or anyone else. So here is what happened after that letter. God answered—just not in the way I expected though.

One Friday after work on June 14th, when I went home, my girlfriend's teenage daughters were having some friends over. I was supposed to go to Miami again this particular weekend to speak, but decided to stay home instead, due to the weather. I was asked to go get pizza for the girls, so I drove over to the pizza joint.

On the way back to the house, a car was in front of me on the street to our house, going about five miles an hour in a thirty mile per hour zone. I honked quickly, but this girl turned around in the backseat and gave me the finger. When I honked again, this time I not only got the finger, but she started mouthing something.

Now this was really not OK with me! In my recovery, I have worked very hard on my angry outbursts and had been doing pretty well up to this particular point. However, for some reason, this situation was making my blood boil.

My program, everything I had been taught and have tried to live, the steps and God started to go out the window fast! As I came up to the street where we lived, the car turned down our street and then pulled into our driveway. I had no idea who it was and I didn't know what they were doing, but I do know one thing—I lost it.

Why were they in our driveway? I got out of the car, yelled at the driver, and then yelled at the girl and a boy in the backseat. Turns out the driver was an Uber driver and the girl who had given me the finger and mouthed whatever to me was my girlfriend's daughter's friend.

I was not happy and I let everyone know it in that car. I'm pretty sure half the neighborhood heard how unhappy I was at that moment. How dare this kid give me the finger and mouth something to me. Didn't she know who I was?

In fact, she did! She had been over to the house when I was there before and was surprised when she realized it was me she was flipping off. I proceeded to enter the house and let every living thing know how unhappy and angry I was about this situation. My girlfriend was pissed—oh, not at the girl, but at me for my behavior at this moment.

My selfishness bubbled to the surface instantly. By this point, I was drunk on anger, resentment, and what I'm pretty sure was unresolved past trauma. I was upset that she wasn't taking my side, and not cosigning my BS. So I packed a small bag to leave for the night, said some choice words, and stormed out.

I jumped into my car and drove to my friend Kurt's ranch house, where I had been staying part-time in between my short stints of home life with her. When I reached his place, I unloaded all of my anger in a rant about how she was out of line, the kids were out of control, and how I was done.

I proceeded to send angry texts to her about how I was mad that she didn't back me up, but she didn't respond. The next day, she sent me a message that it was probably best for everyone if I moved out and not come back. I could get my things the following day.

I was upset, but still felt that I was in the right. All my defects came bubbling up at once. After that Friday, it took about three days for me to come down from those feelings and defects on which I had just gotten drunk. I moved everything out of her house that Sunday. By the following Wednesday, it fully hit me. It was the worst emotional hangover ever!

I finally saw how wrong I had been in this situation. By this time, she wasn't talking to me. I broke down and couldn't even get out of bed. I couldn't remember the last time that I was that depressed.

This was the first time in my recovery that I had truly not felt OK. I knew that I was only running on about eighty percent recovery up till this point. I had absolutely refused to go to any length to correct all my old behaviors in my life. I could talk a good game in the rooms, and walk it outside of the rooms, for the most part. I knew the *Big Book* front to back.

How had this happened? Well, first off, I am human. Secondly, I had refused to look at some serious issues in my recovery journey up until this point. I was OK with having 80/20 recovery. Eighty percent was good and the other twenty percent was something I didn't want to acknowledge. That last twenty percent was like a dent that I had put into a new car. Except "this new car" is a metaphor for my new life gifted by God. This dent was on the rear passenger quarter panel and I know it's there, but I can't see it from my side, so I'm going to put off getting it fixed. The rest of the vehicle looked great.

Before that God email, I had just spoken with a close friend in the fellowship. During that conversation, I laid out a tiny bit about what was going on in my life.

He told me that maybe this pain I was feeling, due to the last things that I was unwilling to review and change, would be great enough to make me change. I didn't think it would be that quick though. The funny thing is, I thought back to that email I sent God, asking him for His help after that conversation with my friend.

I even got mad at God after coming off my emotional drunk. If this was HIS path for me, it's not the path that I would have chosen. In that email, I had asked for help. I even said that whatever HE needed to do for me to stay sober and grow, I would fully accept.

My ego started to deflate and I was in shock—about my behavior towards teenagers whom I'm powerless over and other people's reaction to my behavior, which again I am powerless over, and the way I allowed myself to act and react. That goes back to the only three things I *can* control—MY effort, attitude, and reactions.

I couldn't seem to get out of bed, but when I tried, I couldn't stop getting drunk on self-pity. I didn't leave the house for days. I shut down completely. I tried to go to meetings and couldn't sit in a chair. My mind wouldn't stop racing. Something had to be done.

Then I finally did something about it. I said that dirtiest four letter word to some friends via text and phone—HELP! I was humiliated, because this was the first time in my recovery where I was in an emotional crisis. I had never been in crisis before this. Yes, hard things had happened in the two years prior, but I can honestly say I hadn't emotionally lost it to the point of a breakdown. After I put my ego aside and asked for help, a strange thing happened.

Since I wasn't well enough emotionally to leave the house for a meeting, others brought the meeting to me. As a friend of mine in the program says, "1+1=3." When one alcoholic works with another alcoholic, God is present. It only takes two people to have a meeting. Friends in the fellowship started checking in on me and making sure I was OK.

Now I wasn't looking for sympathy about my behavior in the situation that tangled me into this mess. What happened though is I started to pray harder than I ever have before and then, I started receiving answers. I knew that there were unresolved amends that I hadn't made to previous people. I had made a lot of amends up to this point, but didn't put effort into reaching out to locate other people that I needed to reach. I was kind of letting God bring them to me and leaving it at that. So I asked God for the willingness and help to finish up some major ones. God helped with the assist and amends started being made.

After I made those calls and went to see specific people, I started looking at other things. I really started to look at the possible reasons for my unexpected explosion of anger that Friday in June. I finally put my ego aside and decided to sign up for something that I never ever thought I would be open to—therapy. That was a huge step for this alcoholic.

For most of my life whenever I would get in front of a therapist, I would just avoid the tough subjects or blow them off. Then I would act like my past traumas didn't have that big of an effect on me. I would always freeze up when a serious conversation would start with a therapist, because I felt like they didn't understand me.

My ego was completely deflated at this point. I was fully willing with all of my heart and soul to give it a real try. I was finally open to think that just maybe, I liked to tie past traumas to current experiences. I didn't know how not to. If a relationship would end without me ending it I would feel abandoned so I would abandon partners before they could do that to me. Even if it was just emotionally, I would always check out at some point. So I started really giving therapy a chance.

I also hired a life coach temporarily to help teach me some healthier coping mechanisms. I realized in this moment of crisis that I didn't know how to cope in a healthy way when things in life don't go as planned. Yes, I prayed when turmoil would happen, just as my sponsor and others taught me. Yes, I applied the steps on things and most situations, but that doesn't mean I knew how to cope in healthy ways. I would eat, spend, work, or just avoid things sometimes and then justify my turning a blind eye to the real issues. Because I hired a life coach, I have started to finally learn healthy coping mechanisms.

I started to get real with myself and with my recovery. I began seeing that when my real problems would creep up, real trauma would creep in. Then I would turn away and just go sit in a meeting, mostly to get my mind off things.

During this crisis, I tried to go to meetings, but realized my problems went way deeper than the steps. A meeting wasn't going to truly fix these issues. Only action beyond a meeting would.

Meetings had become a Band-Aid for more deeply rooted things by this point. So I got to serious work on those issues outside of meetings. Then it happened.

About three weeks after the breakup, I couldn't shake the thousand-yard stare from the trouble that I had caused. I couldn't shake the oncoming waves of depression. It was a Saturday afternoon and my gut told me something strange. Out of nowhere, I felt this voice deep inside say to me, "Go to Miami now and everything will be OK."

I blew it off for a short while, but it creeped in again. "Drop everything and go now. You'll be OK." This wasn't coming from my head—it was deeper than that. I knew that voice *very* well. It was the same one from when I started my journey in recovery. It was the one from when I revealed my addiction to my wife in 2022 that said, "Do it now or you never will." It was also the same one that said, "Hollywood," when I was given a choice of either Atlanta or Hollywood, Florida, for my treatment options while I was in the hospital.

I dropped everything, packed a bag in about five minutes, and bolted for the east coast of Florida. My destination was the Stirling Room. I called a close friend in recovery who lived there, said I was coming over unexpectedly, and I asked If I could stay.

He asked no questions and said that absolutely I could stay. I called my sponsor and told him I was coming for the 5:30 meeting. He said he would save me a seat. I called up another close friend of mine who knew what was going on. I asked her to show up and just sit with me. She said yes with zero questions asked.

On the way over, another strange thing happened. My now ex-girlfriend and I talked unexpectedly and we started to have the first real honest conversation we had had in months. We started to lay out where we had fallen short and started to really communicate.

Now this didn't mean we were getting back together, but it felt good to have true honesty back and forth for once. We talked for about an hour during that drive. I hadn't really eaten anything during the past three weeks. During that three-week depression, those extra thirty five pounds I had packed on melted off. I still wouldn't recommend the depression diet to anyone though.

When I got to Hollywood I stopped for my favorite platter of ribs and actually ate something. I got to the 5:30 meeting on time. I walked into the Stirling Room and my sponsor was chairing. The meeting was a Joe and Charlie meeting. I never really liked those meetings before, because we just sat there and listened to whatever tape was played and then shared on it.

However, this time was different though. I was relieved to be at that meeting. After hugging my sponsor, I sat down next to my friend and the tape started to play. The message was Step 12 and practicing AA principles in all my affairs, even at home. It was about how I was powerless over others. I was blown away after that message started.

After the tape was over, my sponsor shared on the same subject. Right in front of my seat was the banner with the steps listed. I couldn't take my eyes off Step 12 and I couldn't shake that message. All of a sudden it hit me where I was truly falling short. All my remaining defects that were holding me back from whole recovery, that I refused to look at in my journey, came to light. I saw them all.

Then my eyes ventured up to Step 6 on that banner. I was truly entirely and fully ready from the bottom of my heart and soul to have God remove them all—root and branch. I prayed humbly to God to remove my shortcomings to help me with these defects. I fully admitted that they didn't serve me anymore in life. I wholeheartedly and humbly offered myself to God right there to build with me and do with me as HE would. My anger and my ego didn't serve me anymore.

Playing God didn't serve me anymore. Being cold and heartless to women didn't serve me anymore. Justifying my behavior didn't work anymore. Being angry at God in times of growth didn't work anymore. They all held me back from being of true maximum service to others in this life. All of a sudden, this rush of peace came over me like I had never felt before.

It wasn't a feeling of freedom like I had before in my recovery. It was more like I felt liberated and wasn't held hostage by my own BS for the first time. I was truly calm. My soul was calm. My heart was calm. My head was quiet. It was TRUE inner peace for the first time in my life.

For the first time ever since I could remember, I felt whole. My recovery felt whole. This went way beyond just loving myself. It was total acceptance of myself and complete willingness to change everything for the first time.

I talked with my sponsor after the meeting and told him what had just happened. He smiled bigger than I had ever seen him smile and laughed even deeper than I had ever heard him laugh, as we talked about the spiritual awakening.

He showed me a passage on a specific page from the book, *Came to Believe*. That page talked about spiritual awakening. It was like I was reading about my own awakening that had just happened. It talked about wanting to die. I really could relate.

During those three weeks, I had fully gone through the five stages of grief for the first time in my life. I didn't numb any of those stages with alcohol or drugs or avoidance. I didn't want to drink or use, but I definitely wanted to stick a gun in my mouth and end things. It was so painful, but then I realized that I was also mourning the loss of what was left of my old ideas and behavior. I knew that I had caused my own misery—God didn't do it. I was letting go completely and it hurt. I knew though that there was one last thing to let go of before going back to Sarasota on Sunday afternoon. I had to let go of Miami. Let me explain.

Miami is where I got sober and found recovery. Miami was also where I went to escape and avoid things recently. It had become more of an escape, rather than being about recovery. I was always looking for something when I went back to visit the east coast on my weekend recovery trips.

I realized also that I was looking for home and closure to the early recovery chapter of my life. I never ever felt at home anywhere—not in Sarasota, not at the ranch, and not at my girlfriend's house, not in Miami and to be completely honest never anywhere ever in my life, not even in my hometown

I always felt lost and never settled. I was always searching for my place to permanently land. Well, I had never allowed myself to be tied down to one spot. Home was where my heart was. My heart was in Sarasota. I was deep down scared of that, so I decided with the help of God's guidance to put that fear away and let myself plant roots in Sarasota.

I talked with my sponsor and let him know about this situation. He agreed and said it was a good thing to go back and plant roots. For once, I didn't feel like I wanted to run from somewhere. I talked with him and he said he would see me when I came over next—whenever that would be.

For once I didn't commit myself to come back to Miami for service, which was actually my escape, but I left it open-ended. During that visit with my sponsor, my close friend, Doc, showed up at the room. I hadn't seen him in months. Every time I went over to the east coast recently, we always managed to miss seeing each other. This time it wasn't a planned meet—he just walked in out of nowhere. We picked up like we never parted.

I showed him my new *Big Book* that was already falling apart and we talked a blue streak. I finally got to tell him how I truly felt about him and everything he did for me in my early recovery. I thanked him from the bottom of my heart and let him know how much I appreciated him. We hugged and then spent more hours talking that night.

He knew what had been going on with me, so we talked about my awakening. We read together out of the *Big Book* and it was like old times. I was able to see other friends that night whom I had kept missing the past few months. It was almost like God had placed them there for a reason. I left the Stirling Room that night, full of satisfaction and joy and that night, I drove to my friend's house to stay, where I slept like a baby.

The next morning, I saw my friend when he awoke. He was special to me, as I had watched him struggle in recovery for months. This time, he had seven months and was doing great. He looked happy and bright.

I had been worried about him for a long time, but I wasn't worried now. It was almost as if he had a new employer, a new freedom, and a new happiness. When we talked, I got this feeling that he was finally going to be OK. There was a lot of joy that morning between us two old friends.

The last time I had seen him was about a month, when he had given me my two-year medallion at the West Dixie. He was a man who Volunteer Alex had introduced me to. I met him in detox when I was speaking there once. He and I had become close. He was always a friend and I even sponsored him for a short time. For once, I felt like God was saying to me that my friend was in good hands.

We went to a meeting together that morning at the West Dixie. At that meeting I was able to see several faces that I hadn't seen in a while. I had always wanted to say thank you to some of them for helping me along the way. After the meeting ended, I spoke with a few of them personally and thanked them for their words and their guidance. In fact, it was every one of the people I had always wanted to thank and had never gotten the chance to do so before. I let each of them know how much they meant to me. Once again, it was almost like God placed them there.

I was able to see the man who had told me those two words that meant so much in my early recovery—"Welcome Home." He said that to me at my first meeting ever at the West Dixie. When he saw me that day, he noticed that I was scared, even with fifty days of sobriety. He put his hand on my shoulder, leaned down as I sat in my chair, and with warmth, love and compassion said, "Welcome Home!"

That greeting calmed me and made me feel very welcome. I kept coming back because of that. I also saw the man who told me, "I like your fire. Don't lose your fire!" I always kept that great suggestion with me. Sometimes in the rooms, you hear fantastic suggestions, as well as good ones, and not so good suggestions.

This was a great one, so I took it. That "fire" turned into the "light." I kept that fire burning, till I needed something more stable and brighter. I thanked that man from the bottom of my heart and we hugged. He is a good man, who helped save my life and motivated me. He is always there for the newcomer and encourages the newcomer in a positive way. He is what the program is about. I respected him always.

Those men also taught me that AA is family and family is love. That's real service right there—motivating the newcomer with your actions, kindness, compassion, and love and helping them to feel welcome and at home. In fact, it was the two of them that told me to write a mission statement in my early recovery. They helped save this alcoholic's life.

Then the last morning meeting happened that Sunday. It was the 10:45 a.m. beginners meeting that Alex and I had loved so much. A good friend of mine was chairing that morning—he's a great guy. I've watched him grow so much in recovery. It was a celebrant weekend, also, so I saw another friend pick up her two-year medallion. We are a month apart in recovery. The month prior, she had asked me if I would be there to watch her pick up that medallion. I told her that I wasn't sure.

Well, looks like I was there now, on this day and that meant so much to her. I was even volun-told to do the chips at that morning beginners meeting. I got up from my chair to walk to the front to do the chips, looked up, and thanked Volunteer Alex silently in my heart before starting them. I handed out one chip that morning. It was a thirty-day chip, picked up by a newcomer. When I asked him his name, he said it was Alex. I smiled big and said in return, "That's a great name. Keep coming back."

After the meeting was over, it started to pour rain outside. I walked out to my car calmly. The rain was warm and cleansing. It was the best rain. I climbed into my car and left North Miami.

As I left the Miami area, I felt at peace even with the rain coming down heavily. As I drove down I-595 onto I-75, the rain kept pouring. As I drove onto Alligator Alley, that Blue October song came on my streaming service. The toll booth to head west appeared in my windshield, which I love. My current sponsor told me once that life was the windshield, and the past was the rearview mirror. I now know that to be true.

I rolled up to the toll booth and paid. The woman in the booth asked me if I was having a good trip. I smiled and said, "Yes." She smiled back such a peaceful smile. As I pulled through the toll booth, the rain stopped on the other side and the sun instantly came out. I felt the door on that chapter of my life close and for once, my hand wasn't in it. I was going back to Sarasota to plant roots and change some things in my life for real this time.

When I arrived in Sarasota late that Sunday afternoon, the first person I saw was my daughter. I picked her up and we went to dinner. We laughed and ate some really good food—my appetite was back! We took a drive after dinner and talked deeper than we had ever talked. She told me some interesting things. I apologized for a few times as far as my behavior was concerned during my early recovery and lately in my recovery.

She really started to open up to me. She told me about when I went to the hospital in May of 2022. She said that she was a deciding factor in me going to treatment. She had told her mom that I shouldn't come back home after the hospital and that I should go to treatment. Turns out, she did know about my addiction and drinking. She even admitted that one time she found my stash of drugs. Thank God she didn't touch them.

I kind of always knew that she knew, but we never discussed it. Then she told me one more powerful thing. She said she was also a deciding factor in whether or not I should come directly home after treatment. She told me that she told her mom that no, I shouldn't come home. That's why I wasn't allowed to come home. Wow-thank you, God.

If I had come right back to Sarasota after treatment, I don't think I would have ever changed or have the recovery that I have today. In a way she is my little savior. I wouldn't have had the journey that I had in recovery, if it wasn't for her. After she told me that, she asked me if I was mad at her for never telling me.

I laughed and had never been happier. I pulled the car over and gave her a huge hug. I thanked her from the bottom of my heart. That little girl helped save her daddy's life, but I never knew.

She is an amazing young woman. She is fifteen and next year, will be a sophomore in high school. She will be driving within the year. Our relationship is better than it's ever been. I'm excited to watch her grow in life. I used to try and cling to her childhood. I missed out on so much of it and never wanted her to grow up. It's almost like I wanted her to go back to being a young kid, so I could get another chance to do things right. I have let that selfish feeling go. I know she will be OK. She can be anything she wants to be in life and I'm OK with that. She is so smart and I know she will do well.

The next thing I did that Sunday evening was to call my friend, Kurt, with whom I stayed with and worked for. I had been afraid for months to tell him that the job at the ranch was taking its toll on me physically and mentally. My body was hurting from years of woodworking. I had tried to switch positions in my career for a long time, but always backed out over the previous year.

Most of it was fear of letting my friend down. I also knew that I needed to leave the ranch as far as living there. I used it as a crutch to fall back on. The doors were always open, no matter what and it was a secure place to land in times of trouble. It wasn't good for my growth. I didn't have to pay rent there. I called him and we talked. I didn't stay at the ranch that night, but instead went and rented a room at a local hotel to sit, pray, and figure the next step out. I took the next day off of work. I went out that day and looked to see what was available in my field of work.

A few months prior, an old work friend had reached out to me about this woodshop that he was thinking about purchasing. If the deal happened, he wanted me to manage it and the staff. The deal never went through, but the current owner of the shop still wanted to hire me for some reason. I met with him that Monday. I guess he had been trying to reach me for the past couple of months. For some reason we never connected.

We connected that morning and he hired me to run his shop and to help change some things there. I was offered a management position and an office. I took the gig without hesitation. Today I love that job. It's more than just a job—it's my new career. I can apply the program principles in all my affairs there and I feel complete in my career. The guys on my team are passing on their industry knowledge to me and I am passing my own industry knowledge on to them. I feel at home there. Will it last forever? I don't know. I am out of the results game these days. All I know is that I am grateful to God for the opportunity and will do my best every day for as long as it lasts.

As far as my living situation, I have moved out of the ranch and into a new place. I feel at home for the first time in my life. I feel like I've cut the strings on any safety net and am able to provide for myself without fear.

Now as far as my love life goes, my girlfriend and I are finally back together and perhaps it will work out, but once again, I'm out of the results game. I'm OK with however things go. I'm not afraid to be alone anymore, but also I am not looking for an excuse to run.

Previously, some of the big problems in our relationship were my work, my living situation, and my follow-through. I never followed through with action afterwards, I would tell her I would do or change something. Today, I don't do that anymore. If I say I'm going to do something, I do it and I also don't blow off plans for spontaneous service commitments in my program of recovery anymore either.

It was drilled into me that we don't say NO to service when someone asks. I call BS on that. Yes, I have service commitments still to this day, but I won't let service disrupt any previous plans I have made, before being asked spontaneously to do service.

Today I plan out my service commitments ahead of time. I also don't attend as many meetings, but I just go a couple of times a week and leave room to work with my two sponsees. It's important to pass on the things that I have learned from others to them. They are willing to learn and I'm grateful to give it away. It's part of the four paradoxes. I have to give away to keep. Just as I had to suffer to get well, surrender to win, and die to live.

As I look at things today I realize that I became codependent on meetings. They are important, especially in the first ninety days. Lately, I had been using them to avoid some of my real life problems and painful, but necessary growth.

Let me explain that one quickly. I can just sit in a meeting all day and talk about living life on life's terms, letting go and letting God, acceptance, prayer, and more. What happens though when I realize I truly don't know how to live life on life's terms? What happens when I realize that the things that I need to handle in life go beyond prayer and acceptance?

We say all the time God can move mountains so I need to bring the shovel, but what if I don't know how to use that shovel? Don't just tell me how to use it. Show me and if you can't show me, then don't tell me. I've had to distance myself and learn how to use that shovel in all sorts of situations. It takes practice.

It's almost as if it works if I work it. Sitting in a meeting and talking about it won't fix my serious problems, if I don't have action behind those words. I need to learn how to really deal with situations in life. So I now turn to others who I know have been through similar experiences in recovery. I ask them for guidance and suggestions.

Real action is my answer now, while leaving the results up to God. I go to Him with everything now and I pause and pray and listen before reacting in any major situation.

What's important to me is practicing these principles in all my affairs at home and in my personal life outside of meetings. I'm starting to get the hang of it finally. I still dive into my *Big Book* daily though. That's important, but it's all important. I look at recovery as a machine and I have to have all the working parts for it to run right.

However, I must still be a part of the fellowship, and I still do service and I keep studying my *Big Book* as I was taught. I always learn something new every time I read through it. My favorites are the stories in the back of the book. As my recovery changes and grows, the stories take on new meaning every time.

I firmly believe that if you aren't reading those stories, then you are cheating yourself. They pair nicely with the first 164 pages, but that's my opinion. The major thing is that I feel that today I am actually living the program of recovery that's outlined in the *Big Book*.

Oh and one last thing—God's got jokes. Here's a good one. The teenage girl who flipped me off that day—you know, the one that God obviously sent to catapult all of this personal change on me. Yeah, I got to make amends to her. I apologized to her and also apologized to my girlfriend's daughters for my behavior, as I am truly doing something to correct the issue today.

I heard a small part of that girl's story and it's heartbreaking. She also had a situation happen at home and my girlfriend is now watching over her. So now I get to help with that, also. It's humbling, but it's also a bright spot in this alcoholic's life. She's a sweet kid and deserves a chance at a peaceful, stable life.

For once, my life is peaceful and calm. I don't feel the urge to blow it up or run or that the grass is greener on the other side, or even that I'm missing out on something. I'm ready to face life head on and apply the steps to it fully. I am awake, I feel alive, and I'm OK no matter what the outcome is in any and all situations.

I'm even OK with any changes in store. I just don't feel maladjusted to life any more. I know that God has my back—it's almost as if I have a new employer. I'm fully prepared to do HIS work well.

Page 77 of the *Big Book* says, "Our real purpose is to fit ourselves to be of maximum service to God and the people about us." It's true and I don't think I was ready to do that until I was fully prepared to meet God in the middle of Steps 6 and 7. I never felt that was possible until my spiritual awakening.

I always wondered when that awakening would happen and searched for it. As it turns out I couldn't "will it," or force it. I just had to be willing to let God work in my life completely, without any resistance, for once. I had to be entirely ready.

Now all the promises in the *Big Book* have come true. I still have a lifetime of work to do to hold on to those promises and also to keep moving forward. It's almost as if this program of recovery is a design for living that works in the best of times and the toughest of times.

What's in store next? I don't know and I'm *not* worried about it. I do know one thing though. My mind goes back to that day in October of 2023, at that corner store. That young man was right. It is better to water that seed with love. Thank you, God.

Printed in the USA
CPSIA information can be obtained
at www.ICGtesting.com
LVHW040121081224
798390LV00009B/754